BROKENWING of an ANGEL

By CARL ERIC WAHLSTEDT

AuthorHouse™
1663 Liberty Drive
Bloomington, IN 47403
www.authorhouse.com
Phone: 1-800-839-8640

First published by AuthorHouse 7/23/2009

ISBN: 978-1-4490-0603-7 (sc)
ISBN: 978-1-4490-0602-0 (e)

Printed in the United States of America
Bloomington, Indiana

This book is printed on acid-free paper.

ACKNOWLEDGEMENT

BROKEN WING of an ANGEL

Inspired by the grace of God, I write and find myself beyond my own capacity that by his hand in mine I place the knowledge written. I am prepared to give an answer to anyone who asks me the reason for the hope that I have.

I find peace includes freedom even from injustice, love and faithfulness belong together, and righteousness and peace kiss each-other.

Book written by CARL ERIC WAHLSTEDT

Cover illustration by BETTY JANE LEWIS

DEDICATION and in MEMORY of:

Karl Wahlstedt-father, Isa, dedrick

Carl Salo-Ukki, dad

Judith Elaine Setala, Wahlstedt, Salo, mom-pikku lintu

Hanna Helena Starck-sister

Rita Elaine Zucccarello-sister

Lisa Alina Wahlstedt-sister

Judy Anita Abril-sister

Dustin Karl Dumas, Wahlstedt-son

Andrew Garret Dywer-son

Tauno and Elsa Karniala-God parents

To Betty Lewis a loving companion and wife, goes my gratitude for her faithful

dedication and support.

To all my inherited family, I love you all.

To God the Father and Jesus the Son of God.

(special thanks)

L.C.Harvick

Brian Harper

TABLE of CONTENTS

COAT of ARMS

WAHLSTEDT

PREFACE

I embrace the fact that question can face answer with understanding.

Questions emerge as DOUBT center stages its stay. FAULT surfaces to bring attention to mishap, and RELIEF visited its partner in faith to know. I noticed REASON swallow its pride to bury its mistake, while ANSWER displayed courage in knowing. QUESTION received its farewell in knowing that ANSWER had fulfilled its doubt by reason and obligation. TRUTH relied on proving false guidance, while HONESTY prevailed with its highest grades. A SENSE of relief re-established a firm argument to face reality, and FAITH above all outlasted any question of doubt that denied its truth. BELIEF sought victory and won, while the SOURCE grew in its strength and exhibited ownership to be as one.

God intervened and became my answer, while BURDEN justified its cause. SILENCE hid in shame, and HUMILITY re-announced its approach, while NEED became who I am today. GLORY sealed its vision, and PURPOSE hosted its approval. DISCOMFORT set aside its differences, paving its security in pleasing its weakness, while ACCURACY now pinpointed by direction released its diversion in doubt, and loss became gain.

In my house from all this Jesus became a household name.

PERSONAL DEDICATION

(To my Dad)

My dreams became wise, yet physically inactive,

Sur-real yet fantasia like,

Meaningful to remember and describe,

The vision burning in my sight,

How I soar with wings of love,

Free within my flight,

Silver rain began to fall,

Sharing the dusting of moonlight,

Rain danced in an avalanche of delight,

Respect to reverence honoring God's most modest design, also right,

Audacious multiples of droplets feared not their plight,

Oceans of shame how profane, endless in time can't fight

Angels cover their faces, as water falls from the sky,

You can rise no higher in concept God answered the question why.

(To start you will now read twelve inspirational picks written by the Author)

(ONE)

God's majestic wisdom, which bathed in its beauty, foresaw the outline and created all that is, and all things were made by him. He reached out in purity and touched the face of existence, as a complimentary design of his reflection produced life as we see it. His nurturing and creative pattern proposed a life form that gave his creation a system of thought based on interests and ideas in humankind, creating all the fundamentals and programs to be experienced in the flesh. The sword of the spirit is the assurance in protecting one's belief in faith that all things were created by him. Also the sacrifice given by his son was to assure the good at heart that all was not lost by the deceit of others. The second coming is the final assurance of rest in and amongst those who choose to believe so. The prophecy in Revelation details the coming of the end of age by his hand, to destroy all that defied his creation in obedience for his love. Willful or not you will taste the end of times and find your result from where you once came.

God save us all.

(TWO)

SILENCE whispered in God's ear, as peace orchestrated mother-natures embryonic beginning. Sunlight danced when God did touch the face of his creation producing a wind so soft as a baby's breath. Air as clean as a fresh cut diamond traveled along the grass that flowed like cashmere, and flowers painted the meadows as birth rose to its occasion.

Like a freeway of independence the territory of shoreline etched its marker of boundaries while holding hands in endless waves of sugar-powdered dunes. Mountain ridges and hilltops sky-scraped the horizon accompanied by a blanket of baby blue sky. Calico underbrush weaved along hillsides to camouflage its crust, and nature's choir sang a melody as a flock of bird's overhead joined in while surveying the showers that washed away worry.

Treasure the moments, match the heartbeat of mother-nature, and feel the pulse of life while your invitation draws to its end.

(THREE)

I lay naked in thought and molested by danger as time approached its final journey. God channeled his silence placing a parade in my view within my sleep of a journey through an underworld of dark private secrets that had their way with me. A mesmerizing image drew me closer to a battle as I sorted out my transmission. I saw disorder and corruption place its vision of disaster below me as I hovered within my cries and shadows like a child aimlessly lost, reaching blindly to where reason outmatched its attack. I was directly above in believing my sight by this slavery, this was Armageddon the day the world stood still as God reached for his compliance to be acknowledged. Mercy for the wicked there was none, impeaching the bondage by putting asunder darker days gone bad, while the noose that bore its burden of evil endured the pain it managed to suckle from un-weaned souls. The upheaval reached its point of sorrow and humility, as suffering center gated its front row seat. I rejoiced in my soul as I danced the dance of God's mercy and compassion to his followers, while my obligation to faith sealed its approval. God then fingerprinted and signed his signature to secure among us the believers our membership to eternal life.

(FOUR)

SECOND ANGEL

My Angel companion tearful in torment aids in exceeding my humility. As I prepare to seek the love she carries within her eyes and share who is buried beneath the pain, I sense a warm and compassionate soul searching for the innocence that is intended for our goodness by faith.

How time in our time has finally connected two hearts torn apart to unite life's purpose to both by the means of affectionate concerning love, truth, and faith, and above all by trusting God's judgment to become one with Christ.

To my wife Betty Jane Lewis

(FIVE)

On a shoreline shaded by a large leafed branch as if God's own handprint covered my thoughts, I felt a breeze so pleasant in wondering, could it be my guardian breathing so close? Cradled in comfort my prayer of hope to come incited my innermost feeling of peace among my fellow members of this world. Concern for the weary and weak displayed its emotion by rain falling from my eyes, and falling short of a breakdown. The depth of my worries involved the core of my being, from cradle to grave, as I earnestly gave my soul to heaven to be cleaned. I reasoned to understand my indecisive conclusion to my inconclusive result by the puzzling thought of how to take back the Holy ground we share in God's creation.

As God began to purify my thoughts to the direction of his word and the message I needed to relay to my fellow man, it became clear that my meaning and purpose of my existence was to service the needs of others.

(SIX)

In my SHORTCOMINGS I fail to recognize them at times and fall short of purpose as I face shame in being unfit by guilt. The duration in time has exposed the decay, which by appearance has displayed itself openly. I caution myself as I walk with care not to shatter another breathtaking incident of despair. Elements of confusion ride my coattails distorting every thought by ignoring my position held as God's child. Lost by temptation and selfishness for personal gain I now wither in my soot fighting back to realize my weakness as survival somehow notifies my demise. Urgency awakens instinct by placing humility in my shadow, and remorse begins to eat my shame, as forgiveness cries from a distance. My illusion of a perfect world by greed has destroyed what means of concern I had to another. I singled myself out to place the remains of my soul on an altar of disgust to plea my case for a possible chance to exist. The foul stench that I had become feels out of place as I crawl to my last attempt at life.

Forgive me I ask, help me I plead, have mercy on the wicked I screeched holding my heart in my hand as my offering beckoned to come together with my God. Soon thereafter I felt understanding and the warmth of his breath upon me, while the moisture of heavens tears embraced me. I knew then my soul had become free of disaster and back in his care.

My father loves me this I know.

(SEVEN)

I BELIEVE I am but of yesterday, and I am nothing but a wandering sheep, strayed and bewildered if not found by my good shepherd as I cry out from my lonesome prayer. A guiding light whispers, who should I say is asking? as its voice echoed in my fear. Then suddenly an amazing harmony filled the air, happy tears, hopeful hope, glorious comfort suddenly appeared. The age of the universe, the breath of life convinces my infinite love. His existence without doubt answers to my defense, while a piece of certainty I find in the guiding light. A sense of serenity and tranquility thoroughly places my fear in justice, acknowledging my needs and providing an explanation of where I need to be. Heavens angelic flock awaits my return and silence glistens with music not of this world. A beauty un-describable surrounds my envy, and passion amplified by grace permits surrender of my will that I can no-longer manage the life I knew.

How pleasant pain is in understanding the sorrow of a lost soul.

(EIGHT)

Sometimes I run with heavy laden, enhanced by chance I think not, yet I question my doubt. Something I long for and desire within my passion is to know myself in meaning, to be firmly fixed by my determination, and to satisfy my position in fastening securely my reason. I lay silent as I examine what is before me, barely visible as time puts my future behind me. I inspect in detail what knowledge I formally need to interrogate my feelings, as I then place what I find to control what I can't see. An expression, a graphic vivid image by mental design assists my curiosity and satisfaction in knowing. I marvel at the information the mind can produce with its imagination, and share only my secret within my eagerness to know. I follow my effort to overtake my persuasion and doubt, engaging only in humor with no harm done to injure myself, as I feed my palate of new ideas.

Kitty-cornered as I look around as far as I can see, only wondering if my extended touch could show me the way. How quiet my life has become in realizing that I could only endanger myself to become extinct. In all actuality my temptation has driven me this far producing this new surge in my view, how complex my thought has become in knowing myself.

(NINE)

As the cry of the wilderness is beside itself, I fear no evil in knowing my place at hand is in the reach God's idea. Willing to plow the seed as one with Christ, I now beseech the understanding I carry, and find peace within my soul. I crave the continuance of my faith and acknowledge the world that has deceived its purpose with most. I now accept and show myself the way to his likeness as I place upon my responsibility the hunger that denied its truth. I enlist my knowledge of him, by him, for him, to the will of his grace, to sanctify the soil of my soul. This overwhelming desire now prioritizes it's meaning to rid the siege by Satan's persistence. This insanity that has rejoiced and relished itself upon greater times has taught me well, as I now treasure every moment God allows me to breathe in his backyard. I now adhere and accept his Will by surrender of all that is to be, and all that is.

(TEN)

My MESSAGE is clear my purpose is to produce the availability and necessity of God's word as he directs the ride. My only reason of self-value I now believe wholeheartedly is to maintain and remain within the realm and justifiable cause in truth, to be true to the glory of God.

Mixed prayers part the meaning created to succumb and yield to his order, while the gift placed upon the cross gave reason to surrender our conscious misplacement. Our communion with Christ relies on our acceptance to abide willfully in the presence of our maker and father of life. Proceed if you will in the direction you choose, but understand that you will no longer have choices at the end. Learn to impart the word at present, give the message of life to those who understand not what they do, and fortify the reliance in God's promise to have and receive the blessed gift of everlasting life.

The reason behind Christ's message becomes self explanatory if the will and desire to reason ideas sets its line of faithful reasoning toward our rightful purpose and intended stay.

(ELEVEN)

Our FUTURE holds itself in God's own time by a healing configuration to remold our spiritual injury, if willing. To restore our spiritual meltdown, healing in the joy of living is now by giving. A spiritual antidote is needed to repair and secure a broken wing by becoming a gatekeeper. Understand Jesus lives, he's alive and I know if I am to walk the shores of heaven and soak my feet in the river of life, I need and require the key.

I have fought Satan and lost, but decided to fight again with God in my corner as my trainer. Victory is close, as my willingness to take the blows necessary to learn where my strength lies in defeating my enemy. I will not accept defeat as I represent and defend my honor to know God. My stability and stamina lies in the foundation of my faith and trust in his Holy power. With this my future holds bright, strengthening every breath I take, as a new chapter awaits me and as I turn the page to my future in God's own time.

(TWELVE)

At our LAST STAND at least I know I will call myself to challenge evil at it's best, as I volunteer myself for all who desire to stand for righteousness sake. I will suit up my armor with the Holy Ghost at my side as I prepare to battle the corruption that fuels my strength to honor my father and his son. I will lead and march on to pursue the enemy of deceit by God's handpicked guardians of his children, and as I pass my way I will recruit an army of deliverance to annihilate all wrongful intent by his promise to a succession of praise. Beware the cross is my sword, the light directs my path, and my faith delivers its plan.

Not an evil soul hidden will be missed as we search under every rock that shadows the darkness that fears our presence. We will feel every heartbeat that exists on this earthly plain until only one pulse remains to be reckoned with and he is ours. God has authorized us to have no mercy as we filter the rubble to expose Lucifer at his best. We face no fear as we carry the key to his place of residence and the chains that we brought to bind his limbs. The seal that will hold his own will carry the weight of the universe by the infinite love that became the root of our victory. Be gone evil one as heavens audience applauds God's victory by his dedicated soldiers of faith.

This next section before chapter one consists of my chosen words expressed by my definitions, to my understanding, to use them as stepping stones or building blocks to structure a foundation as you search your inner self faithfully in becoming one with Christ.

I BEGIN WITH TRUST

TRUST I believe is the custody in caring and having confidence being placed on one-self, this brings forth a firm reliance or a confident belief. Entrusting is to rely and depend on with a sincere credit of value, and to extend the truth to the knowledge of being true confirms your trust. Being trusted unites the wellness acknowledged by one party to another. Being truthful bonds doubt within skepticism by trusting a strong belief in conviction. A sacrifice in putting one's trust first treasures the belief and trustworthy effort in a decision, which takes faith within to believe one another. There is not one too many or one word too few to express all the importance we need in embracing truth at it's best. Be somewhat reserved as you anticipate in removing the opposition to unwanted truth, and before eagerly adopting the face value of it's worth. Remember this; you cannot separate God from truth because he is truth. Being blinded from truth is as to believe in something other than truth, this is as being in the dark. To do the will of God in truth, is his will, and to evade the truth is to become a lie. Remember fear caused by pride to cover the truth sets guilt in becoming a servant of sin.

WISDOM

Romans 1 verse 22: (they who profess themselves to be wise become fools)

WISDOM is putting knowledge to practice. The pain of a hungry soul needs spiritual nourishment and an exuberant understanding in the brilliance of effective guidance. Vital the need, necessary the question, how is it that I thirst when my palate seems sufficient? Not being able to spare any more time to waste my hearts request for fulfillment longs to supply it's void. Appointing my expressed desire for unlimited answers, I now emphasize all interest in an imperial solution from above and within. The crossbar between heaven and earth reflects the journey taken and the path traveled as we aimlessly try all origins of behavior in our development stage. Lessons learned, some not, the want to secure knowledge entrusted in necessity blames only the past. Stabilize your life through wisdom, as it should be, vigorously joining hands with your spiritual guide complimenting wisdom through knowledge, as this feeds a hungry heart and nourishes the soul.

HOPE

HOPE itself is the desire within confidence to fulfill the support in expectation. Having hope, searching for hope, believing and depending on hope excites the imagination of can it be possible, or could it happen, or I wish and pray that what I hoped for might come true. Being hopeful signifies a want for whatever. Hopefully hoping on a hopeless situation sometimes bears on hopelessness. Hope gratifies the urgent need in thinking that some sort of miracle will appear for whatever purpose needed. Through hope faith is born as a silent partner. Within this desire time expects a limit, that an act of faith might produce some enlightened hope. Faith being loyal to hope creates its belief in an allegiance trusting one-another. Although faithfulness is the opposite of hopelessness, they compliment each other due to the fact that one would need the other to work, whereas being hopeful or faithful both work as equal. Your faith in hoping for the best gives the desire to fulfill that expectation of hope that instinctively produces your drive for completion within your faith.

PRAYER

The purpose of prayer is to praise in adoration, to be cleansed by confession through faith, and only then by faith will God receive and listen. When praying, pray fervently be bold and sincere, pray in God's glory and in Jesus name. Jesus said in John 16 verse 23: (assuredly I say to you, what ever you ask the father in my name, he will give you) Any reconciliation to settle differences and to make amends needs a qualifying prayer with no selfish motives, otherwise spiritual harm will address your hearts request. Existing circumstances can sometimes leave prayer as if unanswered. Scripture promises; (ask and ye shall receive) (seek and ye shall find) but as a required condition, God has his reasons in waiting. In Mathew 21 verse 22; (and whatever things you ask in prayer, believing, you will receive) James 4 verse 2 states; (you do have because you do not ask) Prayer is your invisible instrument, so pray according to his will, and remember God's attentive reasoning to follow up and consider all requests are to be by truth and sincerity. Also pray not just for your-self but all who live in spirit, and for the one's who still search for answers. Heal your wounded conscience by prayer and your old life dies, burying past sin to be forgotten. This cleanliness is promised in Jesus name.

Continued

Continuance

PRAYER

Harness your thought prior to speaking to the Lord your God. Prayer can be easy or the most difficult task spiritually attempted. Silent prayer by thought moves emotion and inner feelings that speak for themselves, while his will and purpose speaks for itself. To settle differences and needs your will in exercising choice and need accomplishes nothing without surrender from the heart and to whom the recognition is addressed too. Prayer should be expressing praise first to his needs above all then humbly admitting guilt, shame, and humility from imperfection, this will bring to surface the fear to face that guilt. A release through prayer helps to vanquish burden successfully achieving peace by submitting all ill thought and repercussions in result. Wash your hands, pursue a pure heart, and God will applaud you. There is no speech where he is not present, so ask and ye shall receive in Jesus name. The greatest glory of my life would be to succumb and be accepted.

LOVE

LOVE can take us to the sawmill by being a pacifying weakness, but can also strengthen weakness creating a binding partnership. Love by concern takes loneliness to a level, that sensors the precious moments experienced. With love in some cases comes, the utmost desire of pleasurable intent and the need to erase that loneliness by physical gesture. Love not only exists in partnerships with private intimacy but, vouches for all God's creation. Sacred and spiritual love is the reason why life itself prevails. The source of mankind's emotional need depends on affectionate and passionate concern for one-another otherwise all that exists would become immoral and corrupt. Happiness created from love would be but a thought if not practiced, and would only wander itself in the minds of the just. Love is also a blessed gift that is conceived, when God's blessings are recognized by his grace. Love flows throughout if not seduced by evil manner. I know if we are to expect and receive love we need to be willing to seed love. The best way I can define and describe love is that, love is an alluring appeal that attracts an affectionate magnetic belief, and emotionally your love is your utmost care and concern.

BELIEF

I believe BELIEF is a trusting opinion, or could be a teaching of faith with an established conviction, which could also project to religious beliefs. With that in mind the knowledge beyond our worldly sophisticated mind reverence has yielded this ardent devotion as a belief in all who share a system of understanding of what is to come. Measuring your respect to belief confronts your mirror image in relating to how you believe. In the Christian faith God's palace of praise should be your main objective, calling home through prayer while asking for forgiveness to improve your strength in believing in no other.

The eyeglass engages with the hourglass for your time and purpose. Artificial optimism will ruin any chance of purifying your account with Jesus. Form relations in your belief, spiritually connecting the language barrier in belief to communicate for your defense. Any chance of hope in being acknowledged depends on truth and approach with complete and total submission in yielding to God's authority by your belief in conviction, and being honest and willing to confront him while in prayer. He will know your questions and answers before hand, so do not lie, trust in yourself, have the belief in your message to him who has made all things possible.

APOLOGY

This is one of the hardest, and I agree that pride tends to hold back in addressing an apology. Being ashamed and humiliated by another, leaves degrading scars in a deep emotional state that sometimes last indefinitely. How crucial an exchange is in transferring the shame from the offended to yourself and how it relinquishes the power of hurt. Forgiveness at the same level of respect in accepting is a gratifying emotional relief. The offender releases their feelings of ignorant guilt, while the offended replies with a sense of satisfaction. When pride is set aside an emotional healing permits the experience once devastating and almost unforgiving, now a comment of the past. Erased with concern and understanding care, its final cry of explanation now heard has given its reason for insult and cured by apology. The power of I'm sorry is the hope of curing misunderstandings and a remedy for the ignorance concerning respect.

BEING GRATEFUL

GRATEFUL to be appreciative and realizing how gratifying pleasing can be, the gratification expressed in gratitude is in your thankfulness. Remarkable enough in being thankful creates sisterhood in equal with being grateful. Seize the moment and adopt in approaching a proposal in good faith and accept in giving an emotional thank-you. Surrender on your behalf an expression of good will, fastening need to deed. In approving the understanding in necessity to express a willingness to accept nurtures that acceptance. Furnish the adoration deserved with praise and admiration that gives honor to brilliance. Efforts that recognize a complimentary exchange and then notice the gesture willingly, receives a signal in accepting gratitude. There is an importance in and how one delivers a verbal trade, and the understanding is that giving is as important as receiving. It is crucial to greet in response and to be thankful, and this in itself explains how grateful you are. Learning to be grateful plants the seed of kindness giving birth to a healthy expression.

KINDNESS

KINDNESS trolls its conscience to make way for a compliment to life. Not by passing the pleasure that exceeds it's glory, because I do accept, but knowing that just by being kind deserves its reward. The courtship and relationship that explains the reason for being kind is its sense of pleasing in its motive that produces a calm peace of mind. The comfort in praise by kindness regards the behavior given toward one's concern creating a pleasant arrangement by its aim of intent, and conditions the incision of exchange in kindness.

Some consequences surface at times that are not all in kindness and do validate the connecting frustration. Can tragedy or unfortunate circumstance be kind in defense? I say only God's authority in his decisions known to him reserve the right by his mercy to defend his own, in his kind manner, and by defending his will he preserves that right by cause to save the misplaced no matter what the cost. If ye be kind, kind follows, but to destroy the very gentle thought and nature of its presentation by deceit has its payment. The circle of kindness will be apparent and your share of gentle reasoning will be noticed as God's kingdom regulates to distribute kindness among those.

OPPORTUNITY

OPPORTUNITY is a favorable combination in circumstance and a tendency to expect an outcome. While registering support to any given prospect, housing thought while cradling questions in opinion gives life to opportunity. Grasp all available information to convey in another space and time so you will have the intended result occupy your intended resolution in opportunity. Engross an idea to develop forward progression placing opportunity first. Being aware of your surroundings can present options in availability. Creating opportunity can be achieved by an idea, presentation, location, chance and attitude. The thirst to accomplish your mental conception would drive any encouragement to producing the task involved in relationship to opportunity. A spiritual satisfying occurrence could exist if inspiration makes opportunity accessible. Belief would then inform the influence that surfaces giving rise to a yielding frontier beyond boundaries that exist in creativity. Giving birth to essential cause is to originate a place in time that gradually completes closure from an opportunity if ! advantage acquired in necessity succeeds, and the success in completion to that circumstance circled its way back to reward the effort taken in opportunity.

THE POWER of INNER LIGHT

JESUS is the vision of our invisible God, nourished by the light our darkness can be shut out. Different as we are in our own way, and hidden behind the shadows of our weakness, the power of God's light can be energized within and nurtured till a full glow of its source can be understood. Also believing in the power of authority can compromise in understanding the usage of power, but not as to say using this power to exceed its source for personal benefit or gain, because this becomes a self-centered selfish practice in motive and we all know where that leads. The uniqueness of the power of God when accepted descends in glory to recognize the sacrifice it took to present his enlightened power.

If your pilot light is dim and your source of fuel is low, the possibility of having that light extinguish its flame would then cast its final shadow in darkness, hidden forever without the power of the light. Don't be afraid to go into the light from where you once came, your answers aren't hidden there, its God's place. Follow the power of his guiding light, and once received the power of love will cry out and echo throughout, knowing a thousand horses couldn't pull you apart from heavens embrace.

VIEWPOINT

If the ultimate measure of a man breathes wisdom in sensible solutions and his listening becomes an art form, and the mother of all understanding is his gratitude while respect for God and his fellow man becomes evident, then I believe we have a chance. Ask this question, would your moral excellence rather be ruined by praise or saved by criticism.

We are life's mixture in possibility to reach the divine dynasty intended, so if our deployment of priority collaborates with good intentions to sow the seed by which our determination suits the wellbeing of each-other then this chance does exist. We are by self promise in that our sworn testimony has meaning, and that by webbing our visited idea of Christ's message by his sacrifice can and will offer eternal comfort by surrender, which makes my viewpoint in all its confusion a priority to bring hope from these pages you are about to read over and over again until you understand its true meaning.

God Bless you

THE BEGINNING and the END

In the beginning was the Word, and the Word was with God, and the Word was God. The same was in the beginning with God. All things were made by him; and without him was not anything made that was made. (John 1; verse 1-3)

So as the beginning became so did God's creation of heaven and earth and the design of man to inhabit the earth. The experimental ground and foundation, which was given to mankind was soiled through temptation, deceit, jealousy and mistrust.

Evil had penetrated God's boundaries and shattered all hope for a perfect world. Ancestral sin will exist until the coming of the end. The sacrifice that was necessary to cleanse man and reunite the bond between heaven and earth came at a colossal expense, for Christ's love and death provided a second chance for all God's children.

Revelation 20 verse 15

And whosoever was not found in the book of life was cast into the lake of fire.

Revelation 21 verse 1

And I saw a new heaven and a new earth, for the first heaven and the first earth were passed away and there was no more sea.

INTRODUCTION

This book was written to inspire within all who read its contents, while beginning an earnest search for the truth and hope in faith to carry one's soul home. May its references to scripture and its precious promise be the source of joy in your life, and its precepts be your light. Let the Revelation of God's immeasurable word give everlasting life to the believer, and the assurance to your own personal salvation. Let the beauty of Jesus the Son of God be the inspiration to your own life to be like him.

From here on in you will see that my style of writing is different, my message is direct, and my meaning will be clear to most. Read with an open mind and I believe your heart and soul will find peace. Also this book was not written as a story and delivers no sequence, just thoughts on an everyday basis with suggestion, opinion, and personalized answers written from personal experiences that some say are with a bizarre flare. It is devised to ignite the answer within the questions of what exists, what needs to be done, and how to be saved by Christian values using the author's own personal touch.

CHAPTER ONE

IN A LOST and DYING WORLD

EMOTION deepens as pain becomes evident in need. My un-cleanliness spoke as a voice from afar, which sent its administrator to empty the rubble in my thought. A subtle and keen silence whispered heavens wish as timekeepers of age post a warning to heed to the kiss of eternal death, as heavens spiritual dynasty sorts out existence by precision, digesting and filtering all intent. Anointed by grace, strengthened by belief, and ruled by truth, we march by faith holding high the banner of the cross to those who we found lost. The symbolic symbol that breathes new life for chance lays the cross at your feet in remembering the immensity of his colossal sacrifice for life. Inspired by God's message I share my difficulty to know more. The message says have a listening heart and I will reveal you to you. Desperation remember targets excuses while quoting wisdom has no silence, and I believe peaceful solutions nurture the questions so ferociously asked. I felt blessed when I received Christ in my heart and saw a window above open for me, as it will for you. His decree unto me became alive as I received the restoration and prosperity of my father.

Continued

In this lost and dying world my broken vessel saddened my spirit in knowing how deplorable our kind has become. Only salvation through the power of his resurrection and the fellowship of his sufferings should be agreed upon by his death. A deeply felt and held conviction can wash away sin, heal the sick, and feed the poor and more. The Lord is willing to protect you and give you strength if we are profoundly dedicated in being totally certain and absolute. In Psalm 34 verse 18 & 19 the Lord says; (he is near to those who have a broken heart and saves if having a contrite or repentant spirit) (many are the afflictions of the righteous, but the Lord will deliver them out of all)

Unconditional glory to the soul by Calvary enables the broken vessel to flow with new life giving us the wounded and homesick a passage back home. Deliverance from evil can only be acquired by our true identity to Christ as savior. The outline for life here, and the here after, is in the Holy Bible instructed by God as our manual. Without understanding and practicing the guidelines you will remain lost in a dying world, and miss out on why you were even created.

BROKEN

FALLEN, broken in spirit has its sound witness in necessity, as while dying within our-selves draws a sudden increase for peace that protrudes all understanding hidden in the torment of the living. When you continue to trust to formulate healthy idea by faith and from wisdom used by others, the concealed refuge once hidden in un-healthy idea is justified. Release the suffering placed within your doing, by praying not just for your-self, but to those involved that might have managed to have experienced the pain and anguish created by unfit desire. Their release from this burden will be answered by the dedication of your prayer. Healing is in the capacity to make reasonable decisions, having opinionated idea in discernment and the strength to support the need of renewal.

Angels near and far placed beneath their star,

The message also clear which heaven holds so dear,

Praise in silence echoes so near, keep me from evil, harm and fear.

CEW

TRULY BROKEN

ONLY when you are truly broken are you willing to accept complete change. Watered down versions of past efforts aid only in memory. Brought down without restraint to a level of humble conviction, stripped of honor and liberty, your trust in faith and allegiance for this desire become loyal. To deprive oneself of this opportunity would be insane. The ordeal that has taken you to this point in time can only benefit and encourage your recovery to become sound. When understood the message should be clear in that if you are willing to acknowledge your purpose in life, and that life itself is a gift and privilege, your intended result can now then determine how you proceed from here on in. The apathy in having no interest or living without feeling defeats this rightful goal for our continuous struggle for survival. The answer for inner peace lies in the message of truth and understanding that honesty needs to occupy thought in order to rid the slavery of sin. Involve your-self in service as to become a Samaritan of goodwill and gesture to your fellowman and neighbor. Employ within your heart the true meaning of life and remember without care and concern life is meaningless.

BROKEN SPIRIT

You will see that a broken spirit creates freedom as debt to burden of un-Godly living is freed. The sorrow and agony upon us justifies new growth from our self-emptiness. The broken spirit cries for forgiveness because it is empty and weak. The emptiness when empowered by the spirit defines its weakness, and not by the flesh. This will then start to remold your life by sincerity and love realizing the fact that when you are below your-self a revival begins to take place. The fruit of the spirit is the love and joy within peace that replaces the empty void preserving your spiritual growth and gain.

Remember, want nothing for your-self, the Holy Spirit through our powerful God will see to your needs if your sincerity is true to his word. Having faith and by faith you are saved by him. Faith is a form of surrender yielding possession, while trust is a bond between faith and surrender. Take the desperate measure, prosper and plant the inward seed by choice that you are willing to sow. Refuse to be in a deadlock and use your success as the best revenge to avenge your heart and souls request. Arise in conscience and become a model in motion in morality.

CHOICE

LEARN by choice to restore the religious surplus needed to regain your goodness within God's satisfaction to become whole in the likeness of him. Trust your confidence given by faith to alienate wrongdoing that persists in undermining God's will. The travels taken, some not intentional can be revised and redirected by testimony to your hearts content to surpass and reach further where God awaits your decision. Place your souls sacrifice in front of you, earnestly presenting your-self to prove that your soul deserves attention by his grace. Separated as we have become can be pieced together by the want to live by God's law. Forgiveness sidelines itself until surrender reveals its belief by faith in all that is his. The picture we produce reflects our life and to whom we have relied on to make our decisions.

Be careful, be of wit, and most importantly consider your source of judgment.

ALL WISE

ALL WISE, God is the counsel of his own will and the divine author and authority of the word. Falling out in faith by neglect sends spoils to the spiritual fire burning evermore with increased darkness creating opposition and conflict. When fearful times cast their shadows of disappointment your successor of your will towers the love to clean impure desires and brings peace and excellence to your hearts rescue. Pursue and protect, preserve and refrain from developing the gloom that shares and shades the light needed to flourish. Partake in principle, prepare in purpose, participate in practicing all that is asked and your sincerity will pay the dividends of life after death. To recognize the privilege given by God's authority confirms your trust in Christ and his institution by believing in him, receiving him in trust through faith by grace is your answer. As I mentioned, God is the divine author of the word and the word is the breath of his knowledge and the principles governing his ordinance by procedure and decree, to regulate and rule his mandate by his command for his creation. To live in accordance to God's obedience and in the vision of his understanding, our belief in what was written begins at the heart of his message. The word was and is the beginning now and for eternity.

Continued

Continuance

There is a difference between hearing and listening to the word, as hearing results in learning, but when you listen it's placed beside what you want and choose to do. God's precious word reveals the infinite message of eternal life, and his commandments with given prophecy's through the Holy gospel delivers the history that remains in the lifeline of salvation. There is no future existence or compromise without God's word. When approaching the word make obvious the likeness of him, while solving your spiritual differences in subjection. Relieve the tornacious weight of sin to burden by subjecting all facets of un-Godly circumstance to judgment by God's law, his word. Do not contemplate or devise other means of rule to satisfy personal gain in pleasure, and when summarizing or calculating any ending prepare in its purpose both rules of thumb in knowing how and why being left behind became its answer. Soar in flight, dive in the understanding of life, and the basic root of evil will surface while God hand displays and exhibits the difference. Openly accept surrender by fault igniting truth to vindicate wrongdoing as your soul simmers in its glory.

The thought in memory guides the spirits hand by tasting regret, while ideas of why any of this ever took place is resolved through God's understanding word.

CAN WE KNOW THE NAME of REASON

When you know yourself, deep inside your heart your internal knowledge will compromise to recognize right from wrong. Am I right? Confidentially denying what you widely maintain true needs an everlasting cure. A man who lives a duplicate life practices neither one to its fullest. Deception is the intricate indicator, which weaves spiritual bias and prejudice to influence the state of deceit, perpetrating and committing sin to its devised intent. On the other hand personal growth through pain and adjusting fear forges bridges to bind what has been damaged. I have learned to need or require nothing else, except to settle my differences within my heart and adapt myself to the rightful belonging of my soul. When you are in the position, don't give with one hand and take away with the other, this defeats the purpose to satisfy what was given. To give is to receive and to acknowledge your gift is to satisfy. God has given us life, Christ has given us the way to salvation to redeem our-selves and none will be taken away.

This to me is the name of reason and conviction

NOW

The ABILITY to reason with harsh views and idea, enters the point of question a vast majority of us ask ourselves, how to be honest within reason. Eager and avid enthusiasm to liberate any falsehood sometimes torments the believer in reason, believing otherwise by not being completely honest. The scripture enforces inspiration in operating honesty to test time itself, by upholding the rock of the redeemer. Prayer I find can make concessions to settle any doubt, without becoming a compromiser. A pessimistic view needs attention to improve the privilege of maintaining vigilance within these views. Simple prayer no matter how enormous the undertaking need should place praise first, for this reason, honor and respect to be thankful, which in reason puts the will to want before your request. The reasoning behind this message becomes self-explanatory if the will and desire to reason ideas sets its line of reasoning toward our rightful purpose and intended stay.

The ABILITY within the power to think good sense, gives cause in reason a firm explanation.

THE SHIP THAT NEVER LEFT PORT

The ship maybe battered and the sails maybe torn, but don't let the wind be taken

out of it's sails. Only by un-conditional love in promise will you receive an undisturbed

calm in merited favor, to up hold the spirits desiring possession. The servitude and

slavery that breeds amongst evil desires this possession as a predator stalking the weak.

God's trademark in standard places his foundation as a building block to preserve the

inheritance of one's household. The sacrifice presented by Christ proposes the surrender

of an existing weakness within one's culture, and this we know is the evil welled up

inside our broken vessel.

ATROCITY

Man himself has created his own atrocity, with as much imagination as it deserves, which then goes to say that the instruction you follow creates the future you lead, and that makes you the photograph of your faith. The reality in reason to produce a change in sought idea gives life a chance by becoming an assurance to God's wish. To accept the fact that life goes on is a personal gain, spiritually, and how I express my acute grief is beside me. To bear my burden in sorrow is my vision in priority to improve myself, and I credit my efforts in God's enthusiasm. Eligible for forgiveness I invite my new found faith under conditions of no regret. Undertaking my change caused my intellect insurmountable injury, by the suffering and pain I put upon myself, which quoted my memory thought for thought, distinguishing the error from my good intent. I have never been so insidious that it rattles my soul so, and I found itself least tolerable in pain. The pity I experience as I pass this fear of ruin amongst others certifies my desperation in outcome. The evil opposition has declared war on my soul, while my spirit confesses without anger. My mixed thought exchanges answers to questions that are not given yet, while compulsion inside my confusion tears the lining in my heart separating possibility from reason. The Angels I have disregarded are controlling the impulse to know why, as guilt flew by in horror when I examined my person to resolve my inner misfortune. This brings me to the cry of why.

CHAPTER TWO

THE CRY of WHY

To search thoroughly my intellect polluted by years of neglect, I begin within my feeding ground of availability, discarding old ideas that never worked and dusting off ideas I never tried, giving my unforgiving reason the ability once tried a second chance. God as my witness and I within my fixed limits awaken the need to my wit to succeed my significance to the prosperity of my life. A sign now born of desperation and fear hang loosely on hope through faith, trying to answer the question why.

A build up of bad habits for example need a spring cleaning, which then allows fresh and new entrances to new ideas. No human power alone can relieve the empty blockage of distasteful thought in needing to do what wasn't done. To become one and function as one this requires your full attention and obligation to a higher power that will exceed beyond your question and the cry of why. Cease and pause for a moment, why be anything but his? His fellowship pronounces the peace and relief for existence in closure. Jesus said; I am the vine and you are the branches according to his will, stay connected to the vine, speak the word, be clean by the word, and be the fruit of the word. Confirming doubt, examining thought, produces enlightenment for change in answering the cry of why.

VOICE of GOD

When I ran from the voice of God I found myself devoured by secularism. At this point in time any conceivable option in optimism would satisfy any reason in comfort. Crying from the pit at night I prayed for devout ownership to possess a measure of love, as I hunger and thirst to fulfill my need in spiritual understanding. John 14 verse 6 Jesus said; (I am the way the truth and no one comes to the father except by me) I now willingly submit and succumb to the letter of God by surrender to his will, and by his hand in mine I write and am able to forfeit mine. As you read pieces of my testimony through trial and error, hopefully within these pages your answer lies, either by an answer to a prayer given, or learning by penalty to the promise broken. The red flags of opposition will test your devotion to set apart right from wrong. Send out and receive the blessings deserved if by granting your spirit ownership to be like him. Initiate Godly service to support in teaching the word of God, by placing the Lord on a pedestal of purity in purpose then shed the past in order to move quickly to be like him. Remember him always and he will never leave you, live everyday in his merciful understanding by acknowledging his expectations, producing a promise in by becoming a keeper of his wishes, and a shepherd of his flock.

SILENT MOMENT

A moment so silent as agony unfolds its meaning to life. Confusing at this point it may seem, the journey taken has reached its final approach and your stability feels unstable in thought as it downslides searching for the answer that plummets to physical death. In understanding this, that all that has been created, life itself had death in mind. At this time a better place we contemplate in knowing has loss painstakingly erasing happier times if un-prepared. By faith or lack thereof we proceed in our own visit only pursuing what we had created along the way. Justice will justify the making of our habits and cause will choose by your actions. If by the will of God my meaning is pure at heart I will fear no evil, as time quickens its step with some, others manage a full course in their duty to life. In having a peaceful closure, faith needs to be at work under all conditions. Christians are within the God of my understanding, to alleviate self-righteousness in faithless concern. Destitute for needy change calls desperation by name, holding one's sacrifice for a clear foundation in spiritual growth, while your wounds heal by a mending heart. To avoid self destruction maintain and remain your hearts faithful condition for the service to your soul. What we examine faces our nobility to cause, as judgment races to defend its purpose, and an endless possibility arises searching in quickness to regain ground to know.

Our MORALS become distant, when they fetch every answer available to justify their intent, and when desperation gives thought the limit of idea, infinity touches ground zero with no rightful foundation. In other words, here and there can produce anything from anywhere if the mind is allowed to travel without direction. Caution will teach interest, and the desire to know will give you that one and only answer needed, as your doubt to know defines your request. How about the opposite being, that prediction can only compliment wishful thinking and erase none that had been produced. Placing doubt in thought rides its failure to an underground tunnel of deceit. We charge by anger when we don't understand, we fear the unknown, and we destroy the undeserving will, whereby we find the absolute pain that adjusts to the suffering until we no longer understand our sanity. I ask and wonder what type of creature am I? Who once thought differently but now hinders in the thought of why. To put the image of authority in view surrenders its shield of disappointment and the possibility of bewilderment only excites a fool, while the undercarriage of concern falls short of its sense. Unjust, in being common ground for the weak is where the shale wither while dominant rule prevails and displays its trophy. How far must one go to believe that man himself can change if submittance enters the vocabulary in voluntary order. Helping nurture the character that is injured when all else fails will sow the seed of growth in determining the preservation of life within.

The DARK TEARS a TORN HEART, I release the dragon within, and in doing so my golden years will strengthen and my past life will no longer persuade conflict. Heaven is in you and all you do, so in healing search the joy to make your heart full. The sweet silence surrenders the fear, paving God's geography by an insurmountable abundance of grace. By resurrecting the pleasure within your spirit, your souls good fortune relocates in promise. You will then prosper by acknowledging the passage laid in wake for so long for the reunion of your beginning to end. Aroused in my eager to know I became as a twin in my identity to Christ. My God how I wandered and fell asleep ignoring my purpose and reason for even holding a position to life then.

My illusion of reality has now come to a hold, while my objective has become real.

GROUNDLESS PATH

Yes my WOUNDS are deep, but I have learned to talk to Jesus and by the grace of heaven I will honor God by crusading for Christ. The groundless path I walked upon was difficult alone, as I have now found effective moral power to be victorious in searching the freedom I had once set aside for personal pleasure. I tend to my soul carefully placing duty before my guardian. Watchful as an idle picture setting I move silently by prayer announcing only my pursuit to better myself by God's hand. My heart feels every painful breath I have taken, every wrong step I have required to this day. The mortal suffering, the injury and misfortune that I have encountered, has taught me well. Some scars in memory heal in time, but the deep wounds I have mentioned now have layered protection in my spiritual growth. The arteries of hope flow to my need sowing fertile seed by my faith and the will to live by God and God alone.

HARBORED DEMONS

My soul had harbored demons and insecurities far to long. Apathy the lack of interest or indifference, to empathy the identification of another's feelings, sizes up issues of direct accountability involving the pain and suffering in another's world if one carries blind faith, and that has brought attention to my commitment in this emotional indifference. My neighbor and fellow man deserves the rewards won by my devotion as I replenish my decisions and choices of goodwill, and renounce all my misdeeds accumulated from past repercussions. What I failed to do then now needs to be done for righteousness sake and for my neighbor in order to taste the fortune that awaits our souls inheritance. Jesus wore the stripes of all mans rebellion not just mine, as they lashed out in defiance not accepting the message brought by him. The yolk of slavery to sin exists in the lives of the non-believers choking all chance of deliverance to salvation, rejecting endless possibilities, as their inevitable time will occur. I place my soul in the rightful owners hands and can only hope that my time and attempt to change my fellow mans wrongful ways has erased my human error and acknowledged my plea of forgiveness. Christ's loving glory awaits your decision from the lips of his Angel.

DEATH MARCH

Having BLIND faith is without cause or clear indication in that the weak nostalgia belonging to the past gives instant example of immediate need to implement and carry into effect the drink of the living word. Absolute tenderness, peace, and unconditional love will delight the eyes and heart by simple faith alone. Believe, assert, and affirm to support the blessing of the spirit in receiving this priceless gift. The pouring out of his grace upon the flesh and its restraints enables the Holy Spirit to move freely, healing and producing the restructuring of your soul. Don't allow antagonism and hostility to entrench opposition and institute evil. Constant prayer in one's heart grants excitement in rewarding the pride in healing, as praise in opportunity attracts tremendous steps in accepting the Lords promise, soaring to a higher plain of redemption. Empower his will in permitting the justice deserved, and remember, honesty informs the heart, while the spirit feeds the message.

PAIN, POVERTY, and DISTRESS

Doubt, imagination, jealousy, mistrust, create misery, and is a fine line incurring insanity. Between make believe and what an individual hears, to what they think they hear is sometimes what they want to hear. Is that the doubt within doubt that we have because we have not seen, yet we are led to believe only what we hear that others have seen and written. What presents itself is the lack of faith and trust in and amongst fellowman and his neighbor that creates this topic and exhibits this instability in its insecurity. Your weakness is your flesh, your defense is your spiritual guide and partner and source to saving yourself and all you stand for, as you search beyond yourself for the spiritual identity within you. God created us in his image, while we have created in our own image who we are and what we believe by our actions and desired motives. At the intersection of confusion understanding who we are and who we should be relates our beginning to end. In realizing the fact that we can only be what we create in our mind chases possible doubt in who we are and what we have become. Doubt acknowledges the behavior why doubt might exist and why answers are what we pursue. Don't subject yourself to the physical arena where you believe you are cuddled in safety, instead prepare by your faith to strengthen your weakness in doubt by understanding all the above.

QUIZZICAL or PUZZLED MINDSET

If a quizzical or puzzled mindset is exhibited, this can force a rotation of emotional distress signing one's death warrant. Conveying the means to transform a displaced soul becomes every born believers activity in payment, and this is a spirit driven mission. Our efforts should contain not only petitions for God's continued intervention but also thanksgiving and praise to the hearts of faith. By practicing our good intentions to the best ability we know, then at least this can administer the effort needed to face the fears of evil conflict. Desperation within confusion outside the boundaries of heavens wishes separates the souls divine purpose and postpones the acceptance in the required time to become whole. When hired by God and the call is accepted, be prepared to stand firmly against all odds in defeating the enemy, which orchestrates its detailed plan. God's amazing grace allows us to have custody of spirit through his will and the power to approve our intention. To avert this request consciously frustrates the reflective form we are asked to demonstrate. Essential, our being depends on how we nestle our belief to preserve our right in his office.

TO my CHAMPION

To my champion who was measured, tormented, ridiculed, judged then crucified to satisfy the desperate hunger for religious control. Every imaginable designed doubt and manufactured falsehood represented mans own inordinate and excessive desire. Like a fish without water I ask God to give my withered soul an undisturbed calm. I ask in Jesus name to give me the fearless quality to accept the things I can't change and the knowledge to know its difference.

This next topic and chapter some try to ignore and only discuss in defense or lack thereof. So I wrote this chapter to bring out another side to choice, to show opinionated suggestion within my faith, and to make this chapter a comparable to view your understanding in choice, from atheism, to evolution, radicalism, to sadism and our Christian adversary Islam. In following this chapter I bring you back at the ending to explain my vision and understanding at best as a believer in Christianity. This chapter is the un-pleasant reality of self-indulgence, and that's why I named it the Dark Serpent.

CHAPTER THREE

DARK SERPENT

The serpent of distasteful arrogance bleeds the righteousness from those who fail to recognize, acknowledge, and consume the desperate urgency in need to place the heart of the spirit in supporting our souls rightful journey. At birth our beginning is imprinted in our fathers keeping until thoughtless idea penetrates the innocence carried, and from then on we manage to be eaten alive by irreverent shame. What disturbs me is that in knowing a decision can be wrong or fatal we still waiver the outcome by unfit reasoning. Our life has a timetable and its judgment at journeys end will surface at the appointment. The introduction to life speaks as we travel in time exposing our weakness so closely knitted to our flesh, that we become who we are and how we respond to these unfit desires. We are conceived as a spirit child, but in time we find ourselves divorcing the development of our growth in our spiritual march toward our rightful journey. This un-attended time has misled and misguided our approach in translating and informing our nearness to end. The burden you carry upon your cross will weigh heavy on your soul, and the appraisal you take of yourself can only hinder your chances while experimenting on heavens wishes. No fault of others your choice will perceive you, if not by understanding your place of purpose to settle your differences with God.

DOOMED when self-will finally becomes earth shattering by being spiritually shallow, and the defective intolerable taste of self value summons the execution of your will, then in return your mind misery cites its neglect, victimizing all in its trail. There is no area of dispute you have become a shareholder at the expense of your own design and choice. Self-centered needs have perpetrated the illusive thought of self-will subjecting every aspect and corner of greed in selfishness that perpetration could offer, therefore you have become the perpetrator. The usage of your independent signature as selfishness itself has ruined the spiritual cornerstone in which we as Christians are taught to preserve. Your independent authority with lack of supporting faith has helped deteriorate your reason. Your own reflection casts the blame by your voluntary order of control or lack thereof. When the property of your soul disagrees to inherit what was once sacred and rightfully yours, you have become doomed by desecration. I can only say this, that if you in any form cherish any hope for a better outcome at your final exit, eligibility for atonement only exists if you are willing to humbly surrender your will to the life of Christ.

53

SATAN'S spawn is accountable for all our shortcomings, and its place of power exists in the minds of the corrupt. Short circuit judgment and a repeated sequence of ill offerings are with cost. The might to die for whatever reason exists in the choices of good or evil, and in life we endure personal punishment either way and profit from it by lessons learned or not. Sacred policies crucial to our well being need serious concern by sanctioning wrongful habits and eliminating deceitful resources, otherwise if spiritually dead self-absorbed behavior will prevail. You can make the adjustment and liberate the past by encouraging to discharge evil sustaining thought in affirming Satan's cause by pursuing a conviction and a perspective outlook in defeating the enemy. This then has priority if the will accepts the courage to deny its disfigured personality in character.

I beckon and call by gesture the beacon of truth in order to become one in the eyes of God. As I walk in the valley of the shadow of death I discharge to utter complete and absolute containment of my souls wellbeing to permit my journey to uphold its rightful place. The empathy to share the ability lies dormant until the impulse insists on becoming whole and its meaning to know is reached by fulfilling its final destiny from the obligation desired by God. To reach the pinnacle of my journey I summon all my mannerism accumulated by my earthly proof for payment by my spiritual voucher.

THE DIFFERENCE

SINCE there is so much agitated disorder in the world at present and religious conflict between these two major beliefs, I used the Christian and Islamic beliefs by example to share their difference to understand both.

The Quran reads that Madhi will descend from heaven with Jesus and that Allah is their creator. Also to them Jesus is a prophet not the Son of God, and once descended from above Jesus will serve Madhi.

To the Christian they believe the life force stated in the Bible is the spirit created to dwell within the presence of God, and the connection supports its total being and makeup of Christ as the Son of God. Without Christ and his recognized sacrifice as the Son of God we as his creation would be unable to pass on in our turning point from body to spirit, which Christ provided as savior. The power of the Holy Spirit is to be joined with mans spirit in becoming one through the blood of Christ.

The day of reckoning between beliefs which symbolizes every mans freedom in spirit to wear his crown is believed by Christians that by the sacrifice which God chose in sending his only begotten son, was to place upon his creation his love for man in order to be saved.

CHOICE is what created our sin, and CHOICE is what will save our soul.

EVOLUTION

EVOLUTION to me is a faith of science, a religion of no God, and an authority to no meaning. The reference to evolution defines it as a change of gradual process. I believe that random chance has no purpose or no meaning for life in its highest regard. What are we to do live by political correctness? Then there's theory, principles devised to assume and analyze speculation in phenomena.

I heard the pondering idea of Mars and Earth exchanging meteors billions of years ago, and with the meteorite's came microbes of living cells and under earths suitable conditions these microbes gave birth to the start of life. Instinctively when I know something is wrong, my conscience tells me to head in the opposite corner in idea, sighting if the will is weak, it remains in thought due to the lack of faith.

So to define my evolutionary thought, I have derived with this;
The science of connected thought in theory consists only of definition by calculated risk in guessing.

ATHEISM

A DENIAL of an existing God, and one who doubts the possibility of knowing the existence of God, is an atheist. Some actually hope and pray that there is no God in fear of the unknown. This universal expression in negation or denial is ignorant of the facts, and does not exist in the Christian faith. If there is no God, then that must make oneself a God and a fool in their own moral argument. The study of the nature of God and its religious truth in biblical matters is based in theology and not in optimism, which expects the best possible outcome within doubt.

God apart from us was un-approachable until Jesus came and set the stage essential for mankind to be able to have a relationship with him. The spiritual and physical darkness that we experience with the lack of faith will make us accountable at our final appointment. Jesus came as his father's representative so we could see and not be blind, and believe and dwell in his presence to be assured eternal life.

SADISM in SADISTICAL WORSHIP

Are you a sadomasochist, inflicting pain on others, a believer in spawning poisonous venom by evil malice and ill will, if so hell is your destiny, so be it, do it your way. Spawn and bring forth your unethical morals and choices in principles. Infest what you devise pleasing only your humanistic pleasure. For I know the comfort in sorrow by distress and misfortune, because its hold had placed its practice on me and taught me the difference.

I say bring your hands together, return under God's house, enter in and rid the anguish in your soul. Jesus said; worship is about then and there, and not about the here and now. Devout and earnest prayer will destroy the emotional hangover clearing the way, which is hidden in our worldly worship.

Be the lost sheep that found its way back home.

SHEER STUPIDITY or BIBLICAL TRUTH

Living in darkness describes the solitary separation from light as dim hope.
To ignore truth by darkness is to leave avenues open for Satan to enter in and destroy all control with his desire over your life. Once accomplished the root of bitterness sets in your heart, producing outward hostility in anger that burns as a fire. Your victor over Satan is the only solution and you need not look elsewhere, he is within you just for the asking. At the final judgment your wrong decisions made by choice will have harmed your spirit by having lived in darkness, and the light of hope that lingered in wait for so long has vanished. Accepting Christ at the present certifies your inspirational outlook toward the eternal flame. The Bible is God's salvation and revelation it's historical part true, and its claim honest. Freedom in truth is by his own words when Jesus said; (ye shall know the truth by being true at heart) understanding this explains that the light burns away darkness as peace in the light fuels the embers of life everlasting.

Destiny unbounded by space and time is where we are headed by a guiding light, or if not, the same exists except in darkness.

STUPIDITY

BE AWARE, its here, its everywhere, what is it? (a bubble of stupidity).

Existing by the lack or want to desire the ability to reason creates the behavior of disobedience and then is coerced to captivate an incredible pattern of failure. If the rain showers of faulty repercussions are redirected to navigate a course for a healthy diet in know how, the altered course would then help to avoid an echo encounter in stupidity.

The willingness to understand and prepare for life's obstacles depends on availability in resource, honest effort, dignity, and the courage to want to know. Confronting the hunger to questions and answers that are in a state of unbearable thirst can only encourage the will to learn. Catacombed in your mind the need to explore new ideas renders a prayer for hope that intelligence the desire to know, and its counterpart stupidity the part not willing to try the meaning of learning, would somehow erase that thought.

Suitable surroundings and a reconstructed mindset brings brilliance to the significance of what might aspire.

POST MODERNISM

1 The Bible contains some of the words of God

2 Jesus is the Son of God in the same sense that all men are

3 The birth of Jesus was but an example

4 The birth of Jesus was natural and Joseph was the real father

5 Man is the product of evolution

6 Man is the unfortunate victim of environment and human traits

7 Mans human example as Christ can justify itself by natural development within

8 Denial of Biblical inspiration and miracles to a degree less or greater

9 The Bible is myth, tradition, legend, folklore and human literature

10 An idea of Christ's resurrection came from the grave

11 Jesus will not come again

12 Being able to exercise liberty to force one's license on another

13 The church is a social institution

14 Man wants a social gospel

15 Prayer is a form based upon reflex affect

CHRISTIAN THEISM

1 The Bible is the word of God

2 Jesus is the Son of God

3 The birth of Christ was supernatural

4 The death of Jesus was the atonement for sin

5 Man is the product of creation

6 Man is a fallen sinner from original righteousness

7 Man and women are justified by their faith

8 Accepting the truth of miracles and the inspiration of the Bible

9 The Bible is God's revelation and its historical claims true

10 Jesus physically rose from the dead as taught

11 Jesus will return on the last day

12 You shall know the truth, and the truth will make you free

13 The church is a divine institution

14 Jesus Christ taught a soul saving gospel

15 Whatsoever ye shall ask in my name that I will do

BURDEN

Carefully comparing the burden of my oppression to the percentage of my blessings, my time everyday is a percentage of my earned privilege. I ask myself when tormented by burden, is this anyway to live? definitely no way to die. The answer to this question lies in the value of the burden, was it deserved? what might I learn from it? To act in accordance with the guidelines given, I remember to justify both burden and my blessings in value to understand its reward. We as some are chosen to live as messengers of God in understanding the releasement of guilt in burden, and this affirms to maintain its true identity, while others suffer willingly or by misfortune to search their inevitable certainty. Do not second-guess God, for his fingerprints in certainty are everywhere. As I narrow down my outlook and vision by my past efforts I find my identity is my sense, in that my burden is of my own doing.

THEN THERE is SIN

Galatians 6: 7 & 8

Do not be deceived, God is not mocked; for whatever a man sows, that he will reap. For he who sows to his flesh reap corruption, but he who sows to the spirit-will of the spirit, reaps everlasting life.

Sin is created from the needs met apart from God, and unfortunately the price for sin is death. The gift in trusting God initiates salvation and redemption to everlasting life, which will never be taken away. At your souls request Christ will use a period of time to examine and interpret your inner most thoughts to help develop spiritual confidence to well your heart. The power of God will nurture, discipline, and instruct his will upon you if you accept by proven faith and submission to acknowledge his subscription by your spiritual desire. Being capable of bearing affliction with calmness displays the resistance to fear while trusting his will, this shows him the condition of your appetite, which places his hand in your need. Trusting God arranges answers to questions by divine intervention and develops spiritual endurance creating a lasting relationship to a new and timeless faith. Confidence and stability present ownership back to its rightful owner while peace moves within renewing his message giving the heart final rest and assurance. There is a price for sin, but a wise choice in investment can make the payment in advance.

Continuance

SIN does HURT

Its damaging destructive values are as a black eye.

Spiritual death can be revived, by accepting Christ's offer to join him under a divine and private relationship. Facing eternal separation from God is death, by a devoted life of sin. To exit this drapery of gloom to the promise of everlasting life, Christ presents a safe passage if a volunteer bid to preserve your soul deserves his greeting. Making our spirit alive in Jesus acknowledges his will to follow him in the security of his father. Salvation is the freedom from the bondage and servitude of sin, and this slavery can be paid back in full, debt free, if we assure the adoption to his obedience by promising change. To understand the account opened when turning your life over to Christ insures the riches of his grace and the power within to help preserve the strength needed to sufficiently overcome unhealthy obstacles in evil assembly. A willingness to serve and deserve notice in being an instrument employed by God, executes one's desire to acquire steps taken to an endless position and membership for life hereafter.

Continued

Continuance

ANSWERS become easier when explanation offers the reason for accountability. The fettered restraint and the acquaintance of toxic faith accommodates the traditional rehearsal of sin, and this details the tendencies to restrict genuine trust, earnestly victimizing and cheating the hope in balancing our reality, and this shows by trivial excuses blotting out faith. In reintroducing the application to spiritual authenticity, a vital bond needs to exist in agreement by trust and faith, if the want exceeds its request. If by rejecting all thought of surrender for inner peace, the hearts fellowship in membership to Christ is destroyed. I can only say this that there is a door behind every wall of restraint, and if the key is molded correctly to fit the acquaintance of toxic faith by releasing its fettered restraint, then avenues will exist. Understand once you've received Christ in your life, the only answer to any question lies in his reach.

If you wanted the moon and stars yesterday, it's not too late.

WEARINESS climbed into my soul accessing the security of my identity by Satan's sense of smell. Hidden behind the substance value of material worship the selfish interests had only focused on my needs. The anger and hurt carried far too long had eaten the best qualities shamelessly, and I felt alone carrying the burden of hate within my soul as my endless search brought me to my knees. In time I found faith in myself and now walk the valley of desperation while humility shows pain the way. The cry in my soul notified the tear in my heart, placing the injury in its care. I found that the quest for healing applies the need and exhibits the urgency for survival. When the spirit informs the heart the mind acts upon acceptance, and the soul redirects its purpose. Also when the experience produces the knowledge required for understanding, the pain exercises its awareness by putting shame in humilities corner, and guess what! Helplessness recreates its belief to know, and life accepts a second chance by faith.

EMOTIONAL uncertainty faced with fear measures the power of protection within self-security, as immoral corruption and malignant evil dances in its emotional rule, to disguise this unfortunate weakness. This occupying evil disables the goodness and weighs heavily upon emotions terrifying the spirit and should be surrendered to the will and word of God. When will you be examining your oppression and ill treatment of yourself and others? Self-pity sets for uncertainty and represents un-Godly certainty. To prevail, endure, and challenge thought wisely, invest time by contributing your time to the work of men, and do this in the Lords name. Remember the first will be last and the last will be first, so receive in his good pleasure the compassion promised. On the other hand either you believe or you don't, at the end there will be no sorrow to be expressed, just accountability to your acquired references accumulated along your life's journey. God fashioned his world by intrinsic values and designed moral matters to be obeyed. The chateau in the sky is our earthly cause and ending by choice. This I understand, that debt to sin needs no burden, and an unforgiving heart is a burning separation in your spirit and will corrode and eat your emotional and physical self.

SATAN'S progression and movement by the way of the earth portrays a likely place and image if oneself is unsound and weak. God's image is being mard by its prodigal children every second, everyday. Is it by achievement or obstacle that I recognize the difference? Damaging spoils of everyday abuse deface the fruit of the spirit and disease the heart. The decay in religion that has surfaced in unwanted and un-teachable behavior undermines heavens correctiveness in spirit. God makes it completely clear that in the march of destiny the ultimate price has been given, but wasteful temperament in dishonoring his son has its price. Welled up in my tears what's left of me as I write, I can only imagine how this will end. The grant of immunity and privilege by God's promise holds his grace in waiting, so that we can reinstate our spiritual relationship that will reflect all the good that I have mentioned.

Listen to your heart, feel the beat, and hear the call given.

DEVIL'S WORKSHOP

Isolated like a hermit, having private exchanges of which way to go, I'm a host of my own will. Sinister and evil menace embraces the nightmare adopted by poor judgment that will curse my every motive until I challenge its audience of demons. Resist if you will, protect and defend your inevitable demise, but at least accept failure that has occurred to support criticism in order to recover. Hidden amongst the bowels of indignant pain my traffic of emotions directed on a collision course needs redirection to balance the exchange of impact. The scars that decorate an unhealthy impression can only heal if the right cure fits the package. A living example as myself, drawn between good and evil I burdened myself in all I believed was fair game. Comfort existed until lawlessness brought my attention to reality. The ride I took through the clouds of irresponsibility and self-centered selfishness was not considering the affect on other's, which penetrated my limit of distasteful behavior.

I now find myself in a position in understanding all the above I mentioned, because what I have written became who I am today.

IN RELATIONSHIP TO;

To RELATE to the prior page I should mention that we can only fall when choosing wrongful, or if we agree with the devil. Which end are you choosing, the receiving end, or the giving end? The battleground of the mind reveals the veil of darkness that overshadows the wills desire for salvation. During this time in confusion and instability a door widens and distraction creates chaos in pursuit. The minds medley of balance orchestrates a decision in wondering what choice should be made, and which direction suits its purpose. Understanding the intent relays its message of clarity and focus, surfacing all varieties of possibilities to nurture the outcome by choice. Ask and receive the formula that Christ left in understanding the solution to all life's decisions in truth, and this will reveal the blessing received in surrender by his choice if obligation on your behalf desires peace for the soul.

How far must we go to understand that the answer to freedom lies within, not without.

EVALUATED SPIRIT

As the ever beating beat of the sea regulates its life to be noticed, surely by this awe you believe in some thought of him to discover the simple, soiled, and sorted soul you have become. Yesterday is already yours so what more could you ask for? How about remembering to be thankful by this reward and the blessings of an understanding family. Be dead to sin and alive to God through Jesus, and accept Jesus as your savior and God's temple doors will be opened. Here's my secret to some; God has a gallery where permission has no substitute for victory. (imagine this) A cosmic plantation in a wilderness of joy that explores a forest of twilight, with mountains of possibility that has dancing stars prancing in waves that twinkle in this spectacle we call heaven. Registered truth glistens in this constellation, and catacombs of moons paint a mosaic of meadows where spirits graze in the living word. Grant ownership to your soul, don't take anger to the grave, set aside pride and release the empty pain that poisons your very existence. Be blessed in knowing that we are allowed to speak the very same words Jesus spoke in relaying his message to know we can be forgiven. Remember time is the only thing God will not give back, so time well spent will reward eternal glory by his will and by the desire of his wishes.

LETS NOT demonize reality by demoralizing morals.

WINDOWS of the soul employ information to the struggling mind and heart, in hopes to transform the renewing of the spirit. Search the sacred resources and receive the answers you seek, while the light of the conscience awaits to be ordered. In by caring for other's the thought of goodwill beautifies the nature of divine vision, and forbids any thought of false pretense, in which avoids your adversaries knowing they are your enemies. The spirit would then adhere to the guide and mediator of good intentions, which allows thyself to administer meditation of ill free thought, and replenish the pureness of a calm clean forgiven soul. When sorrow the instrument of learning is blessed by faith, the eye of divine vision and the comfort of knowing sets faith toward victory lane. Support enthusiasm within your drive to know Christ, while the return respect offers the making of all things understandable by the knowledge of his word. The antidote and remedy in truth restores the assurance in the power of faith, which then fosters the right to process and perceive life in its assurance by the power of love.

I SUMMON the inevitable to occur, I approach the final bridge to cross its barrier of displacement. I find no other solution but to reach where destiny provides its answer to acknowledge the ownership of God's existence. I erase the inclination given by those who avoid contact with their soul, and pray that by the grace of God he will provide the means I need to revolutionize the order that persist in evil. I will ride God's chariot to the hillsides to nurture the weakness that prevails in the misunderstanding in our lives. The word will be my source and strength in my faith as I carry God's love to conquer all in its path. Your warning has been given, the signs of days to come have been written. You I seek, and you know who you are. I arrest your soul by God's authority and place your warrant in God's hand. Rewarded and showered by the rain of his glory, my insane views that once vesseled through my veins, now have the company of anointed endurance, which has flourished in my awakening. I have now come to travel with my renewed self and spiritual partner Christ himself. I have overcome my inward pressures between the contest of my world and the kingdom of heaven, and in his kindness and by my understanding his will, I accept the desire within my heart.

My TOTAL FABRIC of existence within my conflicting values has raised an urgent fever ultimately producing my factor in life. Essentially escaping my contrasting ways in which I reflected my being, I no longer postpone my reflection in my spiritual relationship, which to me shares time with my Lord. I discarded my constraints and confinement that took away my care of consulting my inner pressures. I am now obliged by my moral means and am grateful to be thankful for this favor. The opposition had aroused my previous hostility, so I faithfully gathered my aggression which before strickened and appalled my noble cause and my self worth. I realized my extent of harmful characteristics stretching the distance between good and evil. I exploded my rage and yet with calm managed to place my heart here within myself.

Peter 4 verse 16 and 17-(Yet if anyone suffers as a Christian, let him not be ashamed, but let him glorify God in his matter. For the time has come for judgment to begin at the house of God: and if it begins with us first, what will be the end of those who do not obey the Gospel of God.)

My hope to all that linger, I pray that somewhere, somehow, you will find the peace that I now treasure.

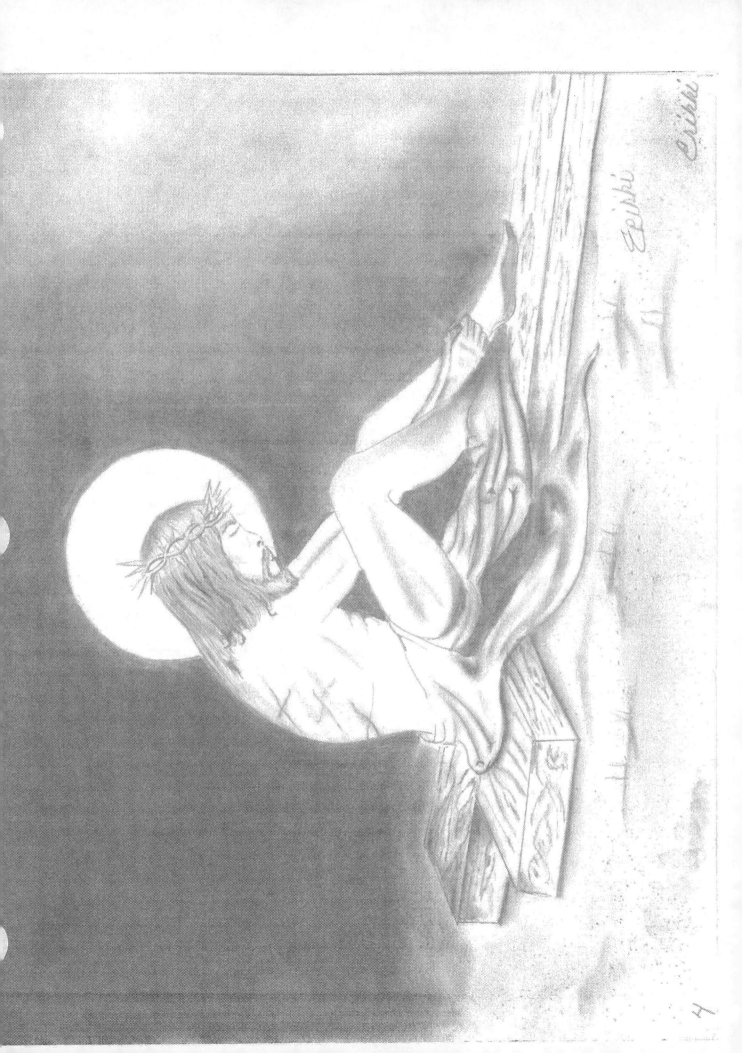

CHAPTER FOUR

MERCY CAME RUNNING

As I study the spiritual origin and development of humankind it placed one of its valued questions in view, can we be saved? Jesus being the central figure and only mediator announces by proclamation that by faith through repentance forgiveness offers salvation. Atonement for the soul and making amends interprets the will of the heart to challenge both the mind and soul's tampered position. To plead on another's behalf when interceding or resolving their indifference, justifies the introduction in pleading the innovation for accomplishment to a sound soul. Blind in mind when born is apparent by the development of his or her unruly principles placed, that affirms the heart's directives and motives, showing that their assumption served justice well and their principles and values were ignored, and remained without change reinforcing evil exercise. Working to become on the honor role of inspiration in spiritual ranking, allows the value of self worth and the principles you stand for to be justified not just for your-self but, in the eyes of our maker.

STEWARDSHIP

We need to become managers in God's behalf. The freedom in following God's plan of stewardship becomes a sincere obligation in harvesting the word. There is no creed or code from the ages of time, only his word. Even as we stray far apart at times somehow we still manage to realize that there can only be one solution that will erase the crisis in desperate need, when we are belly up. Sound humility in humbly serving God helps face the fears of understanding. The will places foresight in the knowledge of need, recycling the past and inviting the future, indulging your responsibility in the truth being his word. Violate not, in placing a wedge in your belief, search for the blessing of the Lord and become a true future candidate in stewardship. Fall in line and illustrate the emphasis in desire to solve problems in God's program, as you use an open heart to confront any backsliding into sin. Fruits of your labor will produce rewards from spoils, and your rainment in his glory becomes an everyday impulse to further your march to spiritual victory.

DO YOU HAVE half the sense in one eye? then one brick at a time is how you will build your new identity for yourself. First being aware of your present unpleasant state can actually release any spiritual illness presenting a new course to salvation. Exactly how and where the occasion suits the decisions made is by trusting all that exists and all that can come to an end. Min-ute as we are, the recognition that has been given to us to be acknowledged by our weakness, was by the coming of Christ. A statesman of glory and of magnificent splendor, he showered his presence then and he remains to this day, to enable the able to reverse their selection from birth till passing, and renew the gift of everlasting life. I use to lay idle in thought as fright in fearing my final rest played out it series, but now his assurance has resurrected my faith. The pain in not knowing is the fear without improving when silence ignores the cry, and while unpleasant guilt injures the condition of difficulty. To re-route my plight, my moral and spiritual power continuously exercises to employ and recharge my faith above all.

Be Blessed, Age Brilliantly

HAVING DOUBT

The endless search for truth relies on doubt, as imperfection was created by man, and whereas perfection was created by our creator. Doubt exists in the minds of those who recreate what they want to believe. Human nature instinctively when in doubt searches for truth by the lack of understanding, whereas religious truth exists in the belief of being true to truth as God's word. In the beginning there was no discrepancy until man intervened by influence to bad choice creating sin, which created the question of what is true. Once the seed of imperfection was planted the divided separation of understanding right from wrong became combatants. How we perceive in what we understand bases its view on truth. Desperation to know serves only the question we search for in our understanding why it all exists, and from where it all began. The physical and spiritual driven uncertainty examines the truth to be understood by reason and explanation. Once understood, truth reveals its source and outcome by only one means, the supernatural creation of a living world by a living and breathing God, the father of creation.

JONN 14 verse 17 (the Spirit of truth whom the world cannot receive because it neither sees him nor knows him, but you know him for he dwells with you and will be in you.)

INCONSISTANT VIEWS AND INFLUENCE

SEEK to be trustworthy, and fair to be firm by accurate influence. What if the opposite was true? The inconsistency to influence any thought or inclination of accuracy sets preference to similarity by being parallel. Minor points of change and variables can and will alter thought. Having accurate occurring influence makes inconsistency an opposite variance. IN OTHER WORDS; similarities in either direction and parallel occurrences influence the outcome even though they are opposite. Intelligible coherence in clear meaning gives exact and correct accountability for accurate influence. Examining thought observes doubt in belief by inconsistent influence, while sensible solutions participate in preparing peaceful confirmation and closure. My point is this, has your past influenced your future, and if so was the influence judged correctly, could have your inconsistent outcome been diverted by observing past mistakes in pride to avoid any observation to already difficult opinion to further complexity. The critical nature presents argument or agreement under an expectation level that permits the power to set goals. Do you want change, and if so seek to be trustworthy and fair to be firm by your accurate influence in your souls desire to become who you are and how you see yourself, this is by the influence you put upon yourself.

Lets Bring It Down a Notch

We need to learn to develop and instruct our good nature to nurture and fulfill the vacancy that exists hidden in our weakness. Because our weakness was hidden a newborn child was born and what captures our heart is how we learn from what we teach by his birth to end. We need to feed the heavenly thirst to obtain the message as he himself taught us.

Worthy Lord is thy name, as you author the words written to lead us to heavenly pastures. Simplify if you will us for those who falter by error, and let us feast and fasten ourselves within the guidelines chosen by your hand, that we might glorify your works to our understanding.

Luke 19 verse 10

(for the Son of man has come to seek and to save that which was lost)

Mathew 9 verse 13

Go and learn what this means said Jesus; (I desire mercy and not sacrifice, for I did not come to call the righteous, but sinners to repentance)

GOD has his HAND in HISTORY lets RIDE

The state of being as one, being active with God and having oneness with God creates endless treasures of spiritual gratification. With this merging oneness the union in divine harmony is as a silent voice whispering in your thought, and his never ending love leads the way by guiding your direction.

Receive willingly and question nothing! Fire the bullet, avoid the unleashing of the apocalyptic flood in failure, and prepare your-self to the ravage of devastation one holds. Life is sacred God provides the security to shun from the destruction of saintliness and the sacredness of life. Gain the spiritual mastery in knowledge to inform steadfast holdings secretly hidden resting in the back of your mind. Expose the evil revealing the wreckage to be salvaged by the goodness and mercy of God's grace, while doing so the pieces of tainted values and principles can now be restored and placed on a mantle of suitable and desirable intent. The purpose in spiritual oneness is that you can experience the glory of God as one within Christ.

CHRIST THE AUTHOR

The author of our faith endured the cross despite the shame against himself for the love of man. We are God's workmanship created in Christ that we should walk with him. We should meditate in his rule of principle and conduct, knowing the fear of the Lord is the beginning of knowledge. Dismantle the pride that chokes us by the scars of sin, justly loving and humbly walking in his presence. Redeem the time unfolding oppression and possession by recovering the voice of expression by the divine.

Provide not take, amend and receive, because to know God is to know Jesus, and to know God is to serve God, and being decisive in his divine expression certifies your relationship knowing the father, while Satan towers in his powers like a wolf stalking his prey, have comfort. Searching for answers in the questions we don't understand is OK! God in his sovereignty has given us his will by assignment and design. We as children of God should in return give to a child of God, this in itself would be as giving to God, and remember a wise man expects nothing in return.

HOLY GHOST

The God given element that contains and protects our wellbeing inhabits the principles and values that are bestowed upon our soul at baptism, so don't punish the loyalty temporarily mis-managed, just prepare to rid all facets of your enemies. The darkness will remain until the light removes the sadness with joy. The despair and troubling doubt will disappear through loyalty by faith and the instrument of purpose will flourish as a spring thaw.

There is a fire of hunger for a new anointing if Christ is in you because the body is dead, by this I mean the law of sin is death while the law of the spirit is life in Christ. Christ became my substitute for sin as he laid upon himself all the sin of mankind claiming nothing for himself but his birthright, he is now acknowledged by all believers who live in his name.

Your spirit in prayer brings into being an obedient heart inseparable to the word.

The SOURCE of my strength is the power of the cross.

To REDEEM myself from the wicked I must clearly state my new view by my intent. Remembering when and how my uncertainty all began seems as yesteryear. The deplorable and scolding blame in my restraint of self-control set fear into the subconscious mind and became subdued by evil manner, which suppressed my normality. I now express the desire to rebuke the corruptible seed I had planted, and won't settle for anything less than God's best.

When I spend time in his word I am correcting myself by healing and delivering the care and caution needed to cure my divided devotion as I am moved by the spirit. I now sense that my body found its sphere of corrective activity and of all things my focus and foremost importance spiritually is to lift up to the joy of salvation. I submit myself and heed to the fountain of fervent and earnest belonging as my soul boldly expresses its security and acknowledges the source of my strength, the cross.

There is no BACKGATE to God's KINGDOM

Who ever HUNGERS and thirsts after him must follow hard, reaching out to the heart of God. Man is the apex of creation, and being so anyone who is in Christ is born as a new creation. All worldly authority bows eventually to death, but an overt and open door is left for those who pursue the word of God for endless life. Break the chains that bind you, release the burden of anguish that keeps the torment alive, then seek and ye shall find the peace that is offered as a gift for your salvation. Guard your heart, and don't be shallow, for once you turn your will over to heaven imagine a joyous wonderland journey as God directs the ride. What more could you ask for with a will managed by the one who made all things possible. Life is a journey a precious timepiece, listen to the Lord in your thought as he moves your spirit and guides your soul.

For God is the before and after, the power that gives strength when all else fails.

THE MASTERS HAND

Jesus became God's match player in a field of disrupt uncertainty.

To change the laws of Moses, Christ released all past regulatory uncertainty by committing himself to sacrifice to bear all burden of wrongful disobedience obtained by sin. Deliverance became reality, and chance became a possibility to save the independent demonic seizure by Satan's rule, which he uses like a terrifying thunder that echoes in one-self frightening the soul and placing a maniacle sorrow in order by fear.

Remember, only attitude faces exposure to deface its character, prying at every crevasse that certifies itself as lame. The web of intimidation, the harbinger of death displays its plan, save your-self realize that where your heart is your treasure lies, and in accepting eternal peace forevermore gives promise that God's grace will allow forgiveness if your will receives your souls commitment to Christ.

Lay it down for Glory, vision a cosmic cathedral pin stripped by geysers of light, surrounded by sizemic pillars of goodwill in an embassy of purity. WOW!

THE DOME of SALVATION

The Holy Mountain, God's Observatory delivers his message by via his satellite to rid the impure motives that bind us in evil. Under God's roof he shelters all who willfully submit to his security in realizing the protection granted by his grace. Remit the careless negligence that persists in resisting his will, and the disbelief and disregard that misled judgment exits by his hand. Since childbirth our foolish behavior has fatigued our innocence in feature by fault that is why heavens legislative body undertakes the harvest of goodwill by seasoning its true patrons. The fragile fragments that had made us incomplete are now reborn by faith in honor, and do celebrate the blessings received from his love. Know that when sin is certain love invades and protects as it penetrates its cause. Love examines life in all things, and God's creation is centered around love with him in mind. We need this caring concern toward love to display what we paint in our life, sympathizing love where it is needed, and your return will be rewarded. The elegance in charm manifests its grandeur in caressing the affection produced by love, while the soul celebrates the blessings received from love.

CARETAKERS

With our hearts in the right place we can find our-selves as caretakers of his will, and in his caring surpass the evil that hovers daily. While pruning the sin that has stunted our spiritual growth we can feed the fertilizer needed to add life by God's hand in manicuring our spirit that rightfully guards our soul. Is your heartbeat just as is? OR is your heartbeat as his? Solemn and formal truth to be as one with Christ enables the promise of salvation and atonement to heal and revise our stay, as we ladle the nectar of spiritual understanding and savor the invitation to satisfy our plea.

Perish all thought of pillaged plunder that robbed and pilfered our goodness, and by pleasing our spiritual appetite now our damaging refuse stored is nothing but pointless time in waste. Precision and significant order by God's hand will refurbish the cloak of the covenant.

FIRE the kiln, mold the pendulum that will flow freely as your spirit reunites its liberty to know God.

God in his own way translates from his purity the meaning of our un-holiness by the power of thought to bring suggestion to replace our ill-mannered truth. As we learn impurities along the way and by inheriting sin from birth, this gives all the more reason to be spiritually aligned in his word and to walk in his truth, while removing the mixed oppression in evil government. We need to raise our-selves even further before him, acknowledging his making and apply the Gospel everyday according to his will.

You know when we spend more time in his presence the character of him and the likeness of his ways become evident. An un-cluttered heart cleansed, and an empowered faith anoints the spirit to fulfill his translation in divine commission. There is an un-compromising supply of God's word available through prayer, love, and down right devotion within your faith. When operating in God's blessings your consequences will be apparent. Genuine prosperity will be yours by your dedication and God's will.

Touch the nerve of spiritual prosperity that combines all creation as one.

The Echo Chamber of Forgiveness

TELL me my Lord all! I earnestly and humbly wish to be another successor of your will. Fold and mold my molecular structure as I face how it was and how it once became my nightmare. Place if you will the parts necessary for me to serve amongst the weary as I know them well. I urge and express the need to salvage those less fortunate who are my distant cousins to this world. The fragments of Lucifer's cabinet have infiltrated those I mentioned and myself included. I beg of you to confine the seepage of distasteful pleasures and corrosive habits of caustic intent bearing compulsion to reason. Help us to merge the hearts desire to the souls purpose in which to create the echo chamber of forgiveness, as we maneuver around the hostile firetrap that institutes and inhabits our wrongful diet. As we surrender a Celestial celebration will devour the rapture of evil investment and your fire escape will have no infinite limits, only an endless cache of glory.

Become a Custodian of man.

If NOT a believer when you start up, your search for the truth might find a level of prayer that might surprise you. Ask for it ! but be careful of what you ask for and how you ask for it. In my quest for answers, my prayer line is my salvation in Christ. When praying, pray not what is only best for your-self but what is good for other's as well. Don't keep your arms closed, but also don't stretch your arms so wide you forget how to close them. Do unto others as you wish done upon yourself, help educate and provide the knowledge that is in the center of God's word. Colossians 3 verses 1-3; (if ye be risen with Christ, seek those things which are above, where Christ sitteth on the right hand of God. Set your mind on things above, and not of the earth. For you will be dead and your life is hid with Christ in God.) Jesus said; (all that the father gave him shall go to him, and he that goes to him in no way will he cast them out)

I have replaced the emptiness with joy and am thankful for another chance for another day.

The HOPE in dying is the reason for living, and in knowing what will take place. The fear of dying is our weakness, in by accepting the fact that life itself had death in mind. When death occurs a sound mind accepts its fact in knowing what is taking place. The distinctive character within a person creates the behavior in thought of knowing that your time spent whether it be to its fullest attentive reasoning or your uncertain success is now at a close. The character we portray explains the individual actions we take, and how we individually understand how we analyze whatever crosses our path. Different as we have become individually relates only to how closely we were knitted, and understanding another's viewpoint at their time of uncertainty or certainty at their final rest gives us the experience of departure in their moment in time. By this event if understood, the experience should release its joy in knowing that the soul has been reunited at the finish line. The sadness is the flesh in its reaction to loss and instinct to the subtraction of one's private possession in connection to a relationship that no longer is available but cherished. The end result should be joyous in knowing that the departed is not held as an earthly prisoner any longer, and if their will surrendered their souls position then they are home at last.

ON THE OTHER HAND

You will only be buried with your name if your soul and legacy left your spirit by denying God's order. Our personalized standards in which our values and principles present them-selves at the end, gives the justification by representation. Attention to God's detailed plan provides his references and guidelines to secure your place in his wishes. While here safeguard the passage needed where solutions exist, and the resolution that is inscribed by devout sincerity. Resuscitate the dedication that has been dormant, and rebuild your faith in God's forum forging your signature in the book of life. On the other hand again, to discredit or cast doubt deprives the hope to believe what was so dearly given. Reach out to forewarn the souls that ache for your understanding, you know the one's scattered amongst themselves in uncertainty, the one's that will create their own unpleasant place of residence. This not occur credit your spirit if your doubt questions your soul, because it is an alarm to notify your spirits wellbeing.

The BIBLE says;

One can put a thousand to flight whereas two can put ten thousand to flight. Tenfold can be obtained by relaying his message within the God of mercy, and in doing so blessed rewards are received. Burning bright the Glory of the father invites your soul to increase in his government, which implements change and order by your service to him. Recruit if only one soul by his word, and Satan retreats one thousand steps backward.

Be the claiming influence, as a well in the middle of the desert, or an island in the middle of the ocean. Stand up, stand out, be noticed, be recognized by tainted souls to enlist the weary at heart. Place hope amongst those whose misguided venture has deceived their trust. Acknowledge those who yearn for the delight and goodness in their heart to know God. Once you have delivered the vaccine of goodness the evil rids itself and you become immune to your once diseased heart. Utter nothing, shout the victory obtained and the resurrection of your spirit rejoices in Jesus Christ.

BELIEVE in no OTHER

On the AUTHORITY by the word I accept Christ within me, and my acknowledgement of his crucifixion to choose death by faith resurrects my walk victoriously in him. To improve thy-self is not the answer but to put back and replace what was lost is. Surrendering one's will lets Christ direct your life and allow the Holy Spirit to live through us. The eternal value of spiritual freedom from destructive emotional strain and physical pressures of life need to be contained in order to inspire change. I gather my inspired thought to believe in no other as his presence signifies my awareness and puts assurance to know he is there. To contemplate is to doubt, and to doubt is to disbelieve in certainty of what is before you. Help knead the dough to the bread of life and help liquidate and dilute whatever ails you in your question. The answers lie within your own reach if willing to amend your broken and torn heart by receiving Christ in your life. Distance not your instinct to know better, but relieve the agony and torment in knowing your souls purpose in God's book of life. The hour weighs well its importance measured by the unrepentant souls and believers. The day is at hand, the time is now, forevermore I am pleased to have found what I had searched for, my endless life. I speak to you in awareness to bring you the news and message that each and every one of you are worth saving. God be with you.

GOD the ARCHITECT

Our loving and glorious God sets a paradigm as an architect to a willed endeavor, (our safe passage home.) Callous and hardened habits have erratically changed our way of living and need more than ever a touch of reality by sincerity, honesty, and not hypercritical content. If willed, rethink to forge a personal touch necessary in pleading for answers that have broken your spiritual wellness. The offer given by heaven to renew and bathe in the veneration of worth reflects our spiritual gain and commitment to complete this obligation. Parent and support by example to others the companion in Christ that you have become, and plant the seed of inward security that nurtures itself while you practice and preach shamelessly your faith in no other. Beneath the obscurity, caution replaces confusion, and rewards become blessed as you savor the highest excellence offered by being dedicated to your faith. Employ yourself as a salesman of Christ rejuvenating revival, as your payment rejoices within God's word. Our life here on earth is temporary, so it be best to understand its full meaning, which will permit an open door to receive the blessed promise in life beyond worldly vision as you travel your spiritually routed journey.

Continued

Continuance

The bounty in spiritual beauty determines its fate by the remission and remittance to sin, relieving the bondage buried in burden that can lead to forgiveness. In pleasing God's table, remember your spiritual parenting and guidance to other's delivers the adjustment in the message that beauty comes from hard times. Polishing our blessed desire relocates the intoxication that once occurred in trial and error, as his seal of approval delivers eternal adjustment that is non-negotiable. The harmony in meditation and prayer caters to his recognition as well as our spiritual maintenance. In the institution of wellness Christ's message is the icebreaker and the blanket from our once sterile diet. Brewing the desire to be on God's payroll gives notice that you recognize that life is not a free trial period, and that your payment is paid either in full or by default. A new found harbor awaits your arrival, anchor firmly on a solid foundation to ride out any storm that life offers by chance or choice. The seed we plant in the depths of our soul will grow by the decisions made. May you find fertile solitude within the season to plant your seed of good intent on God's blessed ground.

Continued

Continuance

Do acknowledge the information in the letters of knowledge and prepare to produce the results that would satisfy thyself and the reasons for others to know, as you familiarize the given words that offer definition by explanation from the book of eternal life. Refine your understanding by teaching all who question the desire to know, and you will compliment God's character by meaning when you take the time to investigate all options of doubt by interrogating the pure result in reason, and by what was received from the letters of knowledge. The vision created in your answer hopefully will supply the understanding to the foundation of your life. Always remember to search for answers within the question, for the answer might lie there, and never doubt the interference of suggestion that might erase your doubt. The pleasing in oneself to know the question in its fullest subtracts the unrest in reason while a gesture of good intent pleases the understanding in receiving the answer deserved by your explanation.

God be with you as you formulate your thought.

I LOOK at opportunity within passing to understand the gift of life.

How prestigious in status one can become in stature if the state of affairs concerning our maker is binding. True to the fact that one who searches for immortality can place upon them-selves a collision course to eternal life. On the other hand, endless encounters of selfishness will test the inner sacredness to evacuate any wholesome interest, so to claim falsely in pretense your faith, trust, and belief then would exceed your boundaries in asserting to maintain you as priority and this is wrong! To repent or regret what one has done, sincerity and true obligation to one's life should have its total attention drawn to forgiveness. This is not a security blanket to those who purposely intend to live life without cause, it is a promise given to those beloved followers who live and maintain a true identity to Christ. All who pass will face the hour at hand in knowing their destiny, and there will be no defense, judgment will be swift and gone as fast as it came. What percentage in purpose do you apply in the employment of God's word? In what direction in reducing your stream of mixed reviews have you found being a participant in assaulting the Gospel? None I pray.

Continued

Continuance

For I tell you this, without being true to oneself and being dedicated to life's intended purpose, the opportunity in passing will only erase what you had created. Death was an addition to life and we live by the thread of existence by place and choice, which takes courage to deny feelings and faith to fear the inevitable result. The emotion to feel is an instinct in human nature and its belief to sense, whereas faith is a supernatural conviction by confident trust and loyalty to a belief in and by whom all things were made. The humanistic character by sense plays its dramatic roll in choice exposing all aspects of weakness in feelings and not in the strength within that exists by faith in its true form of identity. Obscurity hidden in difficulty is distinctly perceived, making one's feelings unclear. Dishonesty sets a base for unfortunate feelings of regret, while truth prepares vengeance in closure revealing the true viewpoint of choice.

TRY THIS ON

I SEEK by mercy the understanding that will recover my garnished heyday in revival. Trumpets of old begin the march at a believers front door, as I am sure not to side step my chosen way. Freeze, then unfreeze the luring temptation, which shadows every call, as by ever so fortunate in wonder he awaits my answer. I manage to put my principles before my personality, and do not keep hostage any expectations. I ice the footage of the past and prepare the present in faith by the love of God. Testimony in fear faces judgment, but I do care to remember that I am my own worst enemy. Any given knowledge can refill the empty void by measuring lost time if space allows the expansion of thought. My learning imbalance troubles the comparison by opinion in choice, and somehow an in-corrective reason applies a hold in its answer. I beg truth in reality to lead the power to think good thoughts by sense, and give its fair and sensible cause the meaning of adjustment, as a stimulant to response. Synchronizing the congestion of suggestion by reason to understand, forces it's meaning in question that is, how, when and why did we become who we are? and where are we headed by the decisions we make? My answer is, the control we yearn for is only by the means of God's preparation and his choice to succeed your will by his desire.

URGENCY by REQUEST

Search deep and gather the makeup of your mirror image that reflects Christ within you. Awaken from the holocaust of your nightmare, and become a groundskeeper of righteous and authentic living while delivering the message of hope to come. Refill the likeness of dreams in your inward pleasure by promising yourself life over death. Be complacent in your honesty, and promote goodwill by service to those who quiver in darkness. Send forth by faith a token of appreciation to all by rendering possessions of no value and demonstrate the urgency to overcome evil that occupies and dwells helplessly by influence, then congratulate thyself in pleasing the Lord and savior by your making. Remember, your personal journey traveled in distance is your lifetime and accounts for your self worth at the end.

God is your tailor of measurement, measuring the purity within your soul as your days have been multiplied and come to an end. (be prepared)

PLACING DISTANCE from DISASTER

By distancing yourself from unfavorable unseen disaster and spiritual difficulty, the reassigning interest in acknowledging the Gospel, is your transforming base to doctrine and the inheritance to your eternal nature. Enable the divine authority to supply its means necessary to support that interest and growth for chance by opportunity. Let God's presence protect you from yourself and all passages of evil. Jesus said; (let not your heart be troubled, he will lead the way).

A priceless passageway, a guardian, and personal guide for eternal life! what gift of comparison could possibly exist to match this existence. Only blind faith could deceive the true meaning of giving and receiving. By the rain of God's glory the freedom of expression lives to defend its right against Satan and his army, who constantly try to suppress and suffocate all in its path by devouring the weak. This is where our righteous game plan comes into affect by reassigning souls to inherit God's good fortune by being his ambassadors and diplomats to faith.

SETTLEMENT

Settle within yourself the unrest by nourishing your spirits craving to be understood as you reinforce the sense of duty by promise in becoming a child of God. In recreating your desire the unforgiving nerve might exhibit its character by shame or guilt, as this offends one's pride creating bitterness of the spirit in a displaced soul. The mixed medly of an unforgiving heart only frustrates a sound melody un-tuned. Indulge in the spirits wishes through God's sacred industry by effortless faith. Prepare and prosper, protect and parent the message given, to amend imperfect solutions. Allow yourself to germinate the seed of fertile solution by faith in trust through God's word. Apprehend any diversion that persists in undermining your faith that is imperative to overcome falsehood. Make a point to appoint within your good nature the change you so desperately need. God is your source of empowerment, play it well and your favorable result in understanding your pursuit will prevail in his will.

God bless the believer.

BEING a BELIEVER of Christ initiates and begins God's use of those who believe in him for his needs as well as our needs. Even demons believe in Jesus Christ and his presence, where are you at?

To accept as true and giving credit to your trust, the realization in determining your result as a believer depends on this struggle. Fight your best fight, and strive to obtain righteousness no matter what, and you will be in the eyes of the Lord a faithful servant and a true believer. Life celebrates its significant event, while reason to some lack a clear expression to define its identity to task as a believer. When Jesus died at the hands of his unbelieving persecutors, all he knew was that the nails had to be driven otherwise all else would fail, and this loving assignment under-minded Satan's persistence through perseverance in spite of it all, and as believers this is the reason behind our faith. For I say to you, all that is by your cause will be as you choose, as you face your final walk where eternal justification resides.

If reckless and unforgiving you will face that reflection, if by truth in being true you will face your mirror image by decision. Forfeit what exists and remains unfit, sculpt and digest his design to reflect his image and your journey with him will be by compassion in concern for one-another which will show by appearance and come to light when God lends his mirror to reflect you in the likeness of him.

CARPENTERS HAND

The BROTHERHOOD created by God's embrace within and amongst our-selves, creates the sisterhood harmoniously placing love for one-another as our guide and struggle to our shortcomings. As I have always cut myself short by sympathetic understanding, I am reminded by sense that all that I need, is to be found in my hearts desire to know him better. Created as equal, we have learned to disperse our ways by temptation in mans desire to prevail by our own needs and not the needs of others. This relationship has caused grief and chaos in our futile existence, while some have managed by the grace of God to withhold from this devious deceit. I have become willing to amend and nurture his desire among all that do desire the empowerment of his will. I place upon myself this duty as I urge every-ones care to know each-others fate by his offer. On the other hand, the artery of self-will in using ones own wishes places perverse and wickedness as a detachable module separating spiritual and earthly contact to the carpenters wishes. This terror in pursuit captures desperation forcing stubborn opposition in compliance to God by ill-full indifference. As a castaway shipwrecked in inner misguided misunderstanding, this ill modification of soul compliance even though still somehow seeks to preserve its keynote to survival. As this cast-net of worldly sin searches for the boardwalk to redemption, the security in his message bridges to bind a resolution in spiritual understanding and forgiveness, which lies in the surrender to the carpenters hand.

I ELUDED MY CAUSE

In the past I eluded my cause but since then have been washed clean by the blood of Jesus, and have been pulled up and out of Satan's den of wolves. Exalted by faith, enriched through love, by my hand I engrave my name in my writing to set aside the dark past, which actually enabled me to search and find a better way. Starved, I neglected to nourish the emptiness, which made me hungry but now realize my craving was the need to know why I am here. My purpose for birth I took for granted, and time not standing still had eluded my cause. Weathered by age and worry, my life at one point in time rode a storm that lasted years beyond my control. With defeat facing my existing years, I frantically grasped my breath as to think where did I go wrong? Panic through desperation put a signal out to alert my conscience that time was running out and the miles of smiles I thought were real were only an imitation and fabricated front. As with this in mind, the happiness that I sensed in my reach now has brought a need to further my ongoing desire to fulfill my life through Jesus Christ.

RIGHTFULLY YOURS

COMFORT relays its message through a network designed by his Holy Grace.

Incomplete as we are, this source ignites the fuel that travels within us to unite the pleasing of our Lord and savior. The desecration and prudence that is our freedom to decide has been manipulated to complicate and distort our direction, while defrauding our purpose of good intent.

Discontentment views the disgrace to honor what was given by being gorged upon by evil. The tomb of darkness lurks in the shadows of an evil empire stricken by deceit, and its principles of ungodly worship. Our heaven possesses the ownership of rescue by our blessed redeemer, and by the sacrificial blood that breathes new life into our injured spirit. Giving away what was not given by goodness alters the network of compliance to God's word.

Come to the table and taste God's glory by the bread of life, I beg you.

MEANING OF THE CROSS

OFFERING self-sacrifice gives life in Christian value the meaning in promise. Self-examination, evaluation of oneself, and confirming the explanation in interest to service others, endures the wisdom needed to be a provider in Christ's name. To evade persecution, and to avoid dark oppression, mercy in its finest hour delivers permissive opportunity in serving God's hand, as festive and favorable faith stands in carrying the Gospel to a renewed and refined beginning. Then by which volunteering this righteous service you enable yourself to reach its highest point by duty. So by saying this, if anticipating any failure there is an ample and sufficient means to avoid self-imprisonment, and this my neighbor cleverly points to a logical cause in purchasing your salvation, by remembering how and why we carry the symbolic CROSS.

THE BIBLE

The BIBLE is the wisdom and knowledge given by God, blessed by his will, then received by man. While God's library has only one book the BIBLE, its testimony of miracles, disasters, beginnings and the end that is to come, is preserved through scrolls and manuscripts that foot notes the scripture of the Bible. The Bible has survived fires, floods, wars through the ages, and is studied more than any book written. From creation to devastation, tragic loss, to jubilant love, the word of the Bible has managed to overcome, educate and direct mankind if he chooses life over death.

The heart and spirit of this book can bring us to the light of the truth, and instruct you to everlasting life. This willingness to listen to his message changes the hearts development to a deeper spiritual understanding within. Extend your arms and embrace God's will, and the longer you practice within the more open your arms reach becomes, and you will find the need to include God in every part of your life.

What a blessing.

JESUS said, what we store in our hearts, our mouth will speak.

Being truthful to who we are takes the step of faith. Am I worthy? Are my debts paid? Never giving up against the raging tide, I will walk by faith in his obedience and exercise my faith. Devotion and compliance will give me the momentum in responding to my faith. I will build an altar unto God, and then will I be able to alter my secret to life. I call upon his name and I know the answer will always be the same, I will give him the glory in the things I need to do, knowing he died for me and you. He came for me with his riches for life, and announced that there is life after death if by obeying all that is his so we can live with him in everlasting life. I willingly receive him with my spirit and can now see my way out of the darkness, as I feel his presence overflowing in and around my spirit while being blessed to have another chance, and no-longer fear myself. I dedicate my lasting impression of life, as God is my witness I search no more.

J Erikki 12-25-16

CHAPTER FIVE

SACRIFICE

UNDERSTAND that you do not live by man's bread alone, but instead by every breath of God's word and only if you are willing to receive him. Do not mock in disbelief, but have a tasteful appetite in decisions, which needs discipline to be effective. Devour your humility, shame, and guilt, and build a new moral and spiritual center pertinent and relevant to enrich the uncertainty in your once collapsed world.

Reveal and expose the unwanted debt to bring into view your violation, which raped your not so innocent identity. Identify distinctly where the pollution exists, and how and why sin captivated and penetrated your soul spreading diversion in unintentional and intentional cause. Show the ability to delegate want in need, which paints your picture postcard of revival to regain vigor in your spirit. Heed to consideration toward others in detail by an attentive desire while understanding why we do not live by man's bread alone. On the other hand, if you sold your soul, you abandoned your values.

The earth will someday dissolve my heart, but my soul it will not receive.

As a STRANGER who became thirsty in likes and dislikes, the conception is the least of these. The perimeters debating the judgment of believers in their likes to the nonbelievers in their dislikes are present by opposite trust. You shall know him by his wants in your likeness of him. His marvelous light will authorize you to be among him, by serving wholeheartedly the amendment to hunger. In realizing the purpose while using his message for another, grassroots the opportunity in saving one's soul. In moving one's spirit forward God himself creates the walk to heavenly pastures. Safe passage by his will utters disappointment to the ex-communicated, while the communicator leads his flock to higher ground. The margin of time remaining points to the lesser desirable creatures dispersed amongst their own. These lesser evil rebels are doomed in a world that is rising in its madness by the rage that will destroy all treasures of beauty, propelled by an orgy of greed and brutality and by the lust for power that will perish by their own hand. As believers we can vision and expect a moment of peace in our time of waiting, as we glimpse the eternal. Once the gates of Glory embrace their own by invitation, the entrance to the invalid will be confined by their demise.

Glory be, as God finally rests in his design.

COMFORT

I CRADLE my comfort by spiritually being practical and while having a close association with believers in identifying myself in Christ. God cleans his fish after he catches them, so I say to this, stare into the window of heaven and channel your spiritual interests for life through Christ, you'll find God's unchanging hands will never let go.

God's infinite knowledge with evidences and certainty welcomes your honest evaluation in his system of truth. The accurate power that directs the direction of comfort relieves and disposes the camouflaged condition of self-imposed righteousness. For me the future that God has in store doesn't rely on past credit gone bad, when forgiven the past is forgotten. Wearing the breastplate and armor with God, shields you from intimidation and distraction, blaming only faith or lack thereof. Being blindsided causes confusion, perpetrating all good intent, while steadfast alternatives aid in resisting negative conflict by passing evil input into the furnace from where it once came. A decision to uphold dignity at its finest, places the soul in confirmed comfort, wouldn't you say?

A UNIT OF MEASURE

There is a unit of measure to be judged by God and the distinction of his Holiness. In Holiness and its regard you need to understand the grace of God and how it is perceived by the intent of his Holiness. In God's view one can play out the goodness in trying to be Holy to create what seems to be unfair, but its existence is to offer even the unworthy a unit of measure in which God allows restoration by submittance. His goodness in Holiness is to assist the trustworthy, and at the same token teach the understanding of a result due to the lack of being Holy. To obtain this treasure in being Holy, consider his wants first to your needs secondary in order for his Holy grace to provide assistance to your wants.

Champion the cause!

What is behind you and what is before you is so min'ute in comparison to what is within you, the Holy Spirit. Work of the flesh is natural, whereas the work of the spirit is supernatural within the power of his Holy Spirit, making it Holy. God is the light of salvation he is the heavenly father, the Holy Father bounded by goodness and good will.

HE is the HOLY of HOLIES.

WHAT is it? It is positively a source of power far and beyond any moral principle in nature and value of human order of control. It is the direct and specific course of action rising above and transcending to exist in the covenant of a binding agreement. Forever real and pragmatic with the facts and actual occurrences, this superior source with its endurance and great value of excellence manifests to rid tortonic complexity within the moral framework of mans error to be separate from it. Beliefs sometimes reveal obvious religious anguish counter binding to associate as one, so the relationship needed to fasten ties in being one with Christ can only be joined by subsequently understanding the following;

Christ's depth of sacrifice in knowing the intense severity of his crucifixion and in seeking peace within oneself and not from without.

I graciously accept in realizing his love for me was not in vain, and his power is the corner stone of my existence.

HOW can displeasure improve itself?

THINK as an example, a cup itself dosen't add to the flavor of the coffee, God brews the coffee not the cup. You can get what you want with a measure of affection due to the fact that the pleasure in receiving is as great as giving. Do unto the Lord as he has done unto us, as with pleasure, and the gift of return can also reward the pleasure of knowing your reward. Can the reward over exceed its pleasure? Only if its pleasure is not shared with its purpose or intent to satisfy the affection, placing the value in its dimension of gratitude. Pleasure prospers with the affectionate concerns of delivery to another, and the acceptance of these rewards pleases the desire in our Lord's wish by placing all as equal, this divine pleasure in pleasing the meaning of its creativity is in the word itself. The satisfaction in the enjoyment of knowing is a pleasurable thought, and to fulfill the relief of doubt within satisfaction can compensate its pleasure.

Preference or a wish in pleasing, explains the joy if affectionate satisfaction is received.

ARRANGE within, and share your love in thought, distract not the remains of goodness, for the extent of which you use spiritual growth to choose gives choice in what was given. No human power can relieve or receive a distinguished spiritual thought unless offered by grace. (God's application is to alleviate synthetic thought.)

True to truth by promise gives faith in thought the pleasure in God's idea. The preference or inclination to think wisely comes from understanding its worthwhile intent by his will. Also the mastermind of knowledge creates the period of question to resolve with answer your thought in idea to doubt. Contemplating stalemates the usage of advancement in thought as excuses neglect the facts, while honesty gives diagnose to its idea. Point made, good intent by righteous influence comes graciously from God's thought, by his idea in mind and realizing life is a succession of moments, pick wisely. Your blessings are wrapped in disguise and in stillness for your hearts content. Being born by flesh can and most assuredly serves evil and lies in some shape or form and at some point in time, whereas born by spirit serves God the father of truth. Christ makes ready our provision to serve as needed by our Holy wonder in spirit, as the word provides solidarity and unity as one with God. To console our religious truth, and to repair and maintain our rightful place, the offering of submittance by yielding to God's authority can and will restore us to a sound condition in our ailing torture. Do we live forever? yes and no, for our souls are immortal and the route we travel by choice is our decision in result.

A PROMISE

A PROMISE is being kept for eternal and endless life, granted if obedient, made by honest choices, and most important serving others honorably by valuing God's most precious creation us. The love we should share should not change with circumstance, but by example. Lets say you noticed someone hungry and barely clothed, and with no shelter, the thought of turning away should not enter your mind, but endure the suffering along with the understanding of their need since turning away would be as turning away from Jesus himself. Love, trust and obey this noble cause and admit to the grief that has tested your inward thoughts. Pray for the merciful grace of God and the Holy Spirit will direct your purpose administering heaven's vision above all to maintain his measure of security by love. Jesus said he will not leave us as long as our faith in him and his father who sent him is our sole intent in understanding his reason.

Peter 4 verse 19- (Therefore let those who suffer according to the will of God commit their souls to him in doing good, as to a faithful Creator.) Peter 4, verse 8- (And above all things, have fervent love for one another, for love will cover a multitude of sins).

EXCELLENCE, SHADOWS PURE LOVE

You will ETERNALIZE in God's foundation by being born of Christ. Proposed by will, announced by sacrifice, and received by love, our eternal sanctuary remains hidden until the doors are opened. God's divine and increasing love is decisive love, a discerning love that is supplied for selfless sacrifice. Purified excellence in love assesses what really matters, but you cannot approve what is excellent until you assess what is excellent, and here's a thought, excellence itself corresponds and familarizes the knowledge of excellence in the properties of purity.

Believe what is to be excellent and your conclusion by mind over mood proves excellence true in removing unstable emotion by pleasing love. Not unwise but wise examines what is best for love, and pursuing love by excellence surfaces the insight to sift the impurities that extract love. Kiss the invitation of excellence offered by what is most significant in God's meaning, and caress to include the adoption of one's love for one-another. A promise for immortality is given by placing love first in hopes of reminding ourselves why we are truly here. Piecemeal this purpose in God's care by putting love in a category by itself and you will love thy neighbor as thy-self, and the window of understanding will affectionately be embraced.

FEELING UNSOUND

WHEN there is a separation between feeling and thought, it becomes emotional in being unsound, and the foundation to the heart is torn by possibly misplacing faith to blame. Example: When there is no direction the course in which you travel lacks function in instruction, so I ask myself how can one be contained in another and lead by faith. I believe we need to deploy our minds to the barriers that bind us. Understanding is to perceive and include the nature of the significance to know, and question the doubt in conviction. Accuracy is to standard, as fidelity is to confidence, that leads a strong rule of faith to an upright belief. Follow the hearts pain be compassionate to understanding, trust in patience and this allows faith to proceed and ones-self to be occupied in Christ.

Trampled by sin of the past and present creates suffering at hand, but the beauty in God's power gives order to the weak at heart, and the misguided and tormented souls that have repented receive restoration to regain vigor in spirit for those who have fallen by temptation.

DOUBLE DOUBT or DESIRE

Your PREDOMINANT importance in understanding the pinnacle point of God's message is to recruit and enlist the slaves of sin. Proficient needs in receiving the flesh to work on the spirit, has God's training program and provisions in order to ascend in his will. If you don't win the present battle the next one might be too late. There is no moral law that can change the heart of man the best method in means taken consciously will result by renewal of self preservation and spiritual awareness by this awakening.

The essential meaning of an aroused and alerted spirit brings life to the heart of rebirth. Doubt will lead mistrust, whereas righteous desire will direct faith to fulfill the doubt in trust. Only faithful obedience gradually signs the signature of sincerity, placing order in spiritual assembly. Comfort to conform and act in accordance to God's law embraces the agreement needed to complete proper fulfillment in establishing a sound relationship in Christ.

JUSTIFIABLE

For every action there needs to be a justifiable reaction. The need and the want separate one another by putting the need first, which is right. To want is more or less a luxury, while the need becomes the necessity for your wants. God is just and the justifier of the just. In putting your needs first in God's care, the unrighteous becomes righteous. I am justified by faith, and when he knows this effort is applied within my faith, he administers and judges my moral correctness. When realizing what is ours is his, these should be offered unto him and in return he grants what is his through blessings.

When we work his message we become one of the same in righteousness. The perfection in him detects and condemns our imperfection, and at the same time supplies forgiveness, so then with this reason the blessed act becomes perfect in his sight and in the favor of his blessing. Once accepted and once the blessing is complete, we nourish ourselves from the act and praise his forgiveness. This act purposely aids the event to change and will salvage your soul to avoid the road blocks in our earthly plain while filling the emptiness with value to your spiritual need.

REMEMBER ALWAYS; you are only rich when you are satisfied within yourself. What you have of material value is only idol worship and of this world. What is gained on earth by face value is worthless and left behind. The amount of worth to worth, and its importance, depends on the price paid for its weight in equal. Rightful purpose per pound outweighs any matter of luxury by the percentage. What you have to loose in shopping at the wrong window is your soul, and what you have to earn and require profits only on the desire of sacrifice. Your advantage in spiritual gain is expressed by ardent devotion and rests on dedication, so balance the only option within your desire that appears to be a loss, and turn over a new leaf for new spiritual gain, and the rewards in return received, present the margin of error. Address fully the foundation of principles you based your initial growth on, then form a self-worth, binding within the riches of heavenly investment, and your revised interest becomes blessed, and you become the richest man on earth.

Second Timothy; Chapter 1- verse-7

For God has not given us a spirit of fear, but of power and love of a sound mind. The power within life must be coherent in mind, orderly and intelligible. When there is no particular purpose or design in your life, acceptability to availability leads to possible post modernism or radicalism, which encompasses a definition without a solid conclusion to a direction in reality building a foundation of regret. Uncover in mind the authentic authority in God where time itself has meaning now and for eternity, and remember that Jesus himself is the benchmark of time itself.

The duration of your stay as a worldly figure by Christian standards relies on faith to proceed, while valued determination is by your actions. We will all perish at one point in time, but to leave a legacy stamped by God's approval is your gift in return to endless life from here on in.

Be not afraid, and bask in your inheritance.

PREVEANT

(Preveant in Greek means; offering grace to salvation and divine righteousness).

I BELIEVE God does not overwhelm or overpower our will it becomes personal. Committed growth in the assurance to walk with God, as he wants us to walk, places confident belief and conviction to truth. The imposter of inward sin feeds the field of failure to omit and neglect the order for salvation. Radical order to abide by deity of deceit is not pardoned or received by heavens court. Heartfelt mourning and sorrow for sin surfaces the fact in truth and we are justified by faith if willing, and born anew as by being preveant. We need to be children of God as we were intended, and we need to be sanctified in the full nature of him while offering self-giving love by being pure at heart. Employ knowledge and continue to practice paying the fee for salvation, and all and more will be added to you in Jesus name.

To withdraw breathes chance, and to restore and revive is as it should be.

JESUS one in alike of the same.

Jesus one in alike of the same, omnipotent and all powerful brings divine inspiration in creating a passage to salvation through deliverance. Accessible by obedience to his word opens immediate nearness, and supplies its eloquent assurance, which endures the understanding introduced by faith. Examination of the soul brings to duty the adjustment of current order by evaluation, entitling closure from a nearby disappointing past. As I search within, a breath to my soul from a prophetic omen warns my determination, by identifying the necessity to include the host of my weakness, while spiritual development undercoats the degree of purification of my unrighteous beginning.

As a mortal mans spirit sometimes betrays its soul by being boisterous and over confident in pride, a cause for crisis suffers for righteousness sake. In keeping faith my ill mannered self has been forgiven and blessed by the exchange of will and visions beyond all righteous imagination. Gone the distant past, the window now open, has aerated itself by pleasant memories and dreams of days to come as I further myself in guiding the purified pain to advance options of never ending pleasure within my heart. I have become God's utensil for saving souls in a battlefield infested with demons, how grateful I am.

IMITATING a precentuious persona, such as pledging to be a true Christian in the eyes of others, while at heart you are only a pew warmer, is as playing golf in the dark. God is in our shadows and knows every thought, intention, and perilous move to hazard our-selves beforehand. As a threat to our-selves and to others is by where we only lead our-selves to believe in what we have personally seen by vision, and not what has been seen by others and documented as their witness to history, (Christ's death and resurrection by example). The selfish nature needs to die in this assumed character, and a purge to purify an individual's artificial appearance needs an exit, in and while doing so impacting others with a newly born spirit induced high.

You've heard the saying divide and we fall, well if true, this would make it your curtain call. Look up John 12 verse 24, Mathew 13 Isaiah 40 verses 21 and 24. Revelation 3 verse 21 reads; to him that overcomes I grant to sit with me on my throne as I also overcame and sat with my father on his throne. (Here's your bottom line) Mathew 7 verse 7, ask and it shall be given to you, seek and ye shall find, knock and it will be opened to you. As the scripture breathes new life into your soul and desire, fill your hunger to know God and you will sample the glimpses of his glory. Hallelujah!

OUR MARCH in time contains the primary priority in sowing and reaping. In our spiritual compass I find the quickest way to seed love is to give love. Families of color are but one as well, and the sunlight of the spirit then can fuel to contain this meaningful precedence. Honor yourself through God's eyes and stow away the undermining persecution of other's. The degradation of an individual or even a community is a demoralization and unjustifiable cause. Arrogant censorship of individual privacy can create disgrace and scorn of oneself bringing about unnecessary articles of personal shame. God's throne of judgment alone focuses on spiritual worth and activity, not to disown an opportunity to save one's soul in need, but to restore the distance in understanding life's meaning and purpose, and to clear the passage regarding love and concern for one another. The respect for thy neighbor gives sound acknowledgement of his request and ninth commandment. If the uncertainty in your spirit is like hurt is to your body then when waking up from sleep dry your eyes and have breakfast with Jesus, and you will no longer thirst nor hunger. Nurture the pain and injury that exists for change by your hunger.

TAKE IT TO THE CROSS

THE HEART speaks to DOUBT, while PAIN notifies the NEED. Feeling empty provides the hunger, fueling the desire to fill the need, which stomachs the pain and nourishes the appetite. Only spiritual fulfillment and a yearning desire for a better way in becoming whole replaces the void, feeding the mind, body, and soul. Reach out, hold on, and don't become a slippery rock once spiritually fed. Grasp the opportunity by inviting return visits from Jesus. (This comes to mind when we have doubt, such as turning to the Lord);

I've been walking with you Jesus, yet I only see one set of footprints in the sand, and his reply would be; the reason you see only one set of footprints is because I've been carrying you! In amazement to myself by the questions I have had in searching for answers in my life, I cringe at Christ's answers that are all so incredible, so precise and moving, that no wit could match.

I find that the more I search from my inner uncertainty, the closer I become who I am.

ARE YOU CRYING OUT? Do you feel rejected and separated from a heartfelt connection within and without? Acquire a new chapter in your life then season your knowledge of God and walk in his ways, by linking the kingdom of God to illustrate your want in his desire. You need a place to go and a direction to take, don't let that space disappear. Reserve the vision and stabilize what is rightfully yours through God's eyes, and implement the strength of prayer vital to the wellbeing of preserving your soul while becoming a privileged partner in the body of Christ. Confide within your heart to encourage the trust by believing in every breath you take shedding the flesh desires while paying a visit to righteousness. For it is in the giving that we receive, and it is in the dying that we are born again to eternal life. Remember we are separated when apart from God, defenseless, divided by whatever unfit craving of flesh desires we create, as injury in suffering designs the debate in behavior through desire. The hidden evil tries to warrant and defend its territory, yielding nothing and surrenders to no one. Addressing this sin invites terror and fear to the heart, but just by believing, the threat permits a cause in alarm to correct the pain in guilt shared.

Being afraid to face the fear by this offensive thought, is the first step in acknowledging your hearts-healing wish to be one with Christ.

MY TRIALS and AFFLICTION I SUFFER with JESUS

I have learned to value my accession by admittance, and let God umpire and referee my heart. I have learned to grow new godly characteristics with the Holy Spirit, which is the fruit of the spirit. I now persist in knowing God's purpose in why he had brought me here. Prayer is what keeps me sound and spiritually whole, being cradled in his love, peace, and joy, while understanding his will and the reason for me to know.

Life has its curves and prospects I say learn to edit a new plan of approval by God's hand. I believe in what I have seen that the poorest are the richest and the happiest, and that the rich are aimlessly unhappy, searching for a happing ending. The pure purpose of happiness solely presents itself if you are willing to listen, and every minute of every hour should be spent living in peace for his glory, as at any moment if not prepared you will sorely be missed. When we stumble it is painstakingly apparent but we can recover if by placing the independent thought aside leaving his Will as your guide. I have done this and found peace, join me.

STUDY GOD

Once you study God and the truth behind him, you will find no matter how faithless we have become he will remain true and faithful. When you decide to serve Jesus, serve him well and you will receive internal discipline in being spiritually useful. To revamp and restore what was once alive and well in your heart, let your blind eye open from the darkness claiming honor to know God. To be justified, revert to your belief in faith, practicing his works that will lead you to a path you would of never known.

Nothing on earth will last and to be content and satisfied in having for your-self profits nothing. If and when you start striving to rid the injury and damage by sin, prudent practical and well-ordered control helps silence your former condition. Enhance your spiritual value, produce in abundance the fruits of your labor, and your entitlement to everlasting life would be as whetting a stone to sharpen your image. Amen

ANSWERS are always hidden within the PROBLEM

Be patient, observe, absorb, and be true.

EVIL rejoices when demonic criticism survives and takes place. God on the other hand celebrates when following his lead, seek his counsel, don't be sidetracked by shrewd reason, which prevails in confusion. Absence from the word not only summons and beckons unblessed results but, reveals unfit circumstance.

A departure from God creates a void separating the relationship as he bids farewell. The deliberating pain that is in dire need needs to realize the morbid and diseased mindset that indicates its final failure by consequence. (This does not have to be so). Instead of an abysmal abyss in a profound depth of emptiness where darkness persuades victory in shadowing all hope, there is a bright side waiting, if in fact your internal desire sets seed to become as one in Christ. Let Christ live in your heart and guide your eyes to understand his Will, and let his sacred and pleasing word reveal the true meaning of joy.

WHO DARES to TALK, WHEN GOD TALKS?

Instinct had dropped him to his knees, while he sobbed in sin breathing as if his last breath depended upon every timeless heartbeat. His memory now warning his soul of crafted deceit that took his pointless life to where he now awaits judgment upon another's feet. A silence carries the answer that sets the platform, which seduced all good at the expense of other's and doubt not even a question of where wrong doing subsequently emerged. How shameful one can expect to become as the baggage accumulated along its journey somehow reaches its close. The possibility of escape somehow ponders even at this moment knowing that the chance for choice was taken for granted and lessons learned if any were never accepted. The voice of darkness gave the illusion of success, but instead created mortal terror in horror to showcase fear at its final appearance.

CEW

5-15-07

FAITH of the HEART

The ocean when turbulent produces cloudy skies, violent and agitated winds, and an unruly appearance on its surface, and slightly below displaying poor visibility and focus. Beneath the underlining surface and underneath all the chaos lie's a calm clear and peaceful setting, a different world. In such case as man by example places in view a similar attitude when unruly.

Our God works beneath the surface setting an inner calm with peaceful solutions. Below the surface in our inner discomforts in understanding, our compelling control to yield to this calm directs the restraint to priority. When facing opposition keep faith in God. Faith is of the heart and faith will voice its desire while the mouth will confess to your belief. Faith also redevelops strength when trust becomes its partner in belief. Understanding these ingredients will calm the turbulence caused by the lack of faith in the heart. God's clear and explicit admiration and wonder for his love is your birth and rebirth miracle.

I AM

YES OLD ONE'S DIE, and new one's are born, but in respect to physical life spiritual rebirth issues a new beginning beyond comprehension. Our glorious redeemer and deliverer, has provided a second chance in the comforts of an existence un-imaginable.

Shoulder your wounds, carry your weight upright, and preserve the truth through Christ's loving eyes. Willingly receive his message walking by his side in heavenly sainthood, while your un-estimated worth in glory becomes your reward. Your spirit will continuously develop and grow by goodness, and your persistent effort will signify the direction aided by the Holy Spirit. Willingly proceed by faith and hope trusting his will and your inner spirits pursuits once declared by Satan's persistence will now secure a position in God's parliament. Your unconditional gratitude deeply expressed by your sincere thankfulness for life's treasures here and beyond, will reunite in reunion your soul with the one who sent you at your journey's end.

TO TEACH is to explain the understanding and make it clear.

TO PREACH is to relay the message already clear that needs to be taught. The level of our holiness exists as it endures all persecution by placing our ill weakness in suffering that was once un-forgiven, at the feet of Christ. Bearing burden to bad choices that had directed our genuine intentions of good intent gone bad, has been removed by the cross. Our living God has offered to take our surrender in by offering his will. Our newly born purpose assigned gives proper promotion in distributing the message of the Gospel. Demonstrating repeatedly the true meaning of the word satisfies in applying discipleship in his glory. Being captive and then freed from evil bondage guides the living spirit as a witness to his message. Saving souls provides opportunity to serve and preserve what could have been lost.

As the 99 sheep lay still, the shepherd should be willing to search for the one that went astray and rejoice above all for finding his lost sheep. We as Christians can benefit our own peace at heart while assisting the nurturing of hearts torn between good and evil. How pleasing it is in knowing that the goodness served to others also nurtures your own peace of mind by placing your willingness to serve the will of God.

HEAVEN'S POSTAL CODE

Waiting in the midst of old are the elders of revival, and the warriors of the word.

In the un-ending vision of God's extension itself is a living reality in the here and after.

The sacrifice given on your behalf by love qualifies the vacancy left in waiting to be

fitted and filled by the righteousness of his will and an endowed spirits desire. The course

traveled by Christian faith, bases its trust and confidence in conviction to accept as true

the credit in faith and congratulates its reward by the above. Life lived in the flesh I now

live by faith alone. The honor in honesty relays the word of Christ, and to the scriptures

given by God based on faith to both. The evidence of self-commitment escorts the

purification of one's soul in the amount by which one enters the treasure trove of heaven.

One will find this plateau elevated to a precise and accurate gift of Holiness, where love

exists and endures all persecution, pain in suffering and shame on Christ's behalf.

THE CHRISTIAN HERITAGE and TRADITION passed down from generations concerning the religious ceremonial right known as the sacrament, has been invaded in some by silence. The righteous formula has been disregarded and its strength of disaster entered by force as well. In order for its betrayal to succeed, faithless loyalty in its purpose can dominate one's holdings in hope.

WHY oh WHY do we go so far as to let the only meaningful resolution or pure result pass bye? Without sight in reason, a hidden ending in catastrophe will determine our destruction and fate. The intended blueprint in living true to the gift of life can be embraced by the only source available and sacred to this cause, love in our living God.

REDEEM your-self and save your soul, and recover ownership by obligating worship in praise for salvation and debt to sin. Inherit a new beginning within your faith, trusting your savior and creator above all. Involve dedication to righteous deeds by including members of the past and future. Passion the un-limited and never ending need for redemption to service, by his glory in Jesus name.

CHRISTIANITY not INSANITY

NOT elected but assigned by the divine desire and authority of God's command, the armor of the Holy Ghost by God's expression delivered the Holy Spirit and had Jesus come live in my heart. For all my days prior to partially being dead to sin and wise to my belief, my faith and trust has now overwhelmed my spirit, and the righteousness of my concern to humanity relies on spiritual support to place trust in his majestic wish.

ALIVE in spirit is to be recharged in the word and to use this practice un-selfishly in the presence of his authority, while gathering within to encourage one's spirit.

Requiring this relief and assistance to further avoid physical, emotional, and spiritual neglect, allows his wisdom and guidance to escort your needs to pursue life here on earth, as he demands.

THE MESSAGE

The heart of the Christian message is the cross.

LEARN to bear the punishment within the burden of your souls restoration, and search for answers in obedient effort, by placing your desire in his presence, and delete all evil idea in the remembrance of him, and you will taste the sweet nectar of life everlasting. Also learn to criticize what seems evident in the eyes of evil, and do not submit to disgrace by choice, but assist your souls need in repentance in order to establish the regret or penitence for what was failed. To squander time by postponement reflects your worth devoted to views that have become pointless. The cultural cross symbolizes the message in earnest regard for restoration, and makes available the opening to become burden free.

Host a free will in accepting the Lamb of God by choosing not to walk in the path of sinners or sit with the scornful, but exceed to righteous persistence, while restoring what was taken away and to what was so dearly given.

CLOSURE

THE COMMITMENT to Christ in life points a believer to reverence in electrifying unquestionable investment in time and closure. By illusion reality builds a wall failing to do what is required and in not realizing there you are, not what you claim to be. There is no grey area, just black and white. Join the living without resistance in understanding the engineering of change embodied in accountability, morality, and charity in Christianity.

The viewpoint in representing spiritual quality within, gives the essence of divine harmonic peace throughout our supernatural thought. Remember God is everything he is the beginning and has no end. His mere gift in understanding his design of worship is our line of communication to know him better. Put aside delinquent desires and inspire within your heart the relationship promoting his will in your understanding.

AMEN

CHAPTER SIX

FINAL ANSWER

Give us this day OUR DAILY BREAD has always been misinterpreted.

What this means is, the bread of eternal life is given by the Father and offered by his Son, for whoever believes in him will have everlasting life. The bread of Christ is he himself who came down from heaven and gave life a second chance by earthly sacrifice unto himself for those who would choose life hereafter. Jesus is and became the bread of life and says, he who comes to him will never hunger, and he who believes in him will never thirst. Also he who believes in him will never perish but have eternal life.

He that believes is not condemned but he who does not is already condemned. The will of the flesh is not without sin, so find rest within your soul and your blessings will flow. The heavens were created by his infinite wisdom and the world was proven by his knowledge. While he is now and as before, search him while he is close. Be abasive and humble and ask only for his needs in praise treasuring all that is and all that has been given to you.

God be with you always.

WONDEROUS DREAM

As the ANGELS choir revealed their clarity, the communication became pure and the heart secured its purpose in knowing its value to each-other.

Awakened by a thought that gave the persistence of unrest in its reason and explanation by means not of this world, I contemplated its significance that channeled its instruction by certainty in greatness. I only questioned my difficulty in reaching the quality of this superior deliberation by its certainty in undermining laboriously the product of our suffering. I now see this map to heaven that consists of stars that are the eyes of Angels, and that this heavenly body sustains to filter the souls symphony that orchestrates its composition by the degree of truth. While evil the masquerade that retaliates against the simplicity and purity of devotion by its message of personal pleasure in becoming more important than the truth in the eyes of the beholder, actually presents its relentless, pitiless, and persistent provocation in design and leaves no alternative in God's constitution. Loyalty to follow faith by obedience in representing pertinent and germane convergence will find the pathway in identifying his Son's identity to the soul within. To know God is to appease God, and to know Jesus is to acknowledge his message portrayed by his ultimate sacrifice.

NOTHING DONE WELL is DONE ALONE.

Imprisoned in my own skin without cause or care is the result of my decisions, which has drawn in an uneasy emotion overriding reason. My curiosity sparks a new direction in helping to assist in my conclusion that derives from self-judgment. My, imprint of suggestion autopilots instinct in depicting achievements by personal examination. Opinionated or controlled influence behind my impulse to visualize accurately the message grimed and gaunted by determination, tests my confidence to know. Somehow I sense spiritual relief as God peace-meals an antidote while at the helm.

He might ask, are you worthy of my time? while attending to his perfection at its finest. Equivalent to none, or equal value to no power, I submerge as I submit in knowing, that Jesus could have called upon a thousand Angels at his time of suffering to take his place. I place my hand in God's palm to decode my regrets and know I am worth every breath I take. My honor is to know God, my blessing is my loving family, my gift in life, is my God fearing spirit, and my position held in my new understanding is that I have become a soldier of Christ and a warrior of the word.

I am pleased.

GOD LIVING THROUGH ME.

We are so afraid to die because this is all we know.

The scripture provides the answers of what is to be expected and what is outside the limits of our earthly realm, as some are still guided to believe otherwise by searching elsewhere. The departure from the flesh is not the end but a beginning. Our creation as equal will not be as one until we've reached our final destiny, and where the space and place in time shelters our unbounded residence of eternal rest for all who have acknowledged the kingdom of heaven.

Our responsibility and accountability is not to exert effort into self needs, but to yield our desires to our fathers will and allow him to live through us. Spiritual fulfillment at heart discovers life and the pleasure of reliable authority in him once you have received Christ. To seek the absent cure while reaching further in his understanding is to resolve and preserve the redemption of your soul.

BORN AGAIN in SPIRIT

When there is discovery for the lost, recovery for the injured, or strength for the weak, this thrills my soul. Development in change in taming the torment is not just for sheltering our own desire to become whole, but investing in others becoming holy and blameless before him, as if building a fire against the cold while exchanging the cross for your crown. To grow or come to be as one in the mystery of God's will joins his infinite search in saving souls. Jesus came to surrender for all humanity's sake, rendering his life by sacrifice whereas representing hope for all human order.

Understanding the Gospel and its description of reality has put new order in my life. I find that the future excellence and assurance in success is by God's un-exhaustible torch that burns as an un-divided light, promising stability in the meaning to destiny, and I can only follow where my heart leads in knowing that his will is my life.

My interests no longer burn to the desires of worldly possessions, since there is no storage at heavens gate.

AGREEABLE to the WORD

When agreeable to the word, a solemn promise with a positive affirmation sets sail in faithfully planting the seed of the Gospel while you build a relationship beginning in trust. Your sacrifice in service lends credibility to the message of salvation and the work needed by a secure and entrusted belief. Firm reliance committed to care will gather and harvest a forthright appetite for future hope. Liberating and sharing the sorrow of past darkness offers structure in sheltering and protecting the delivery of your spiritual victory and exultation.

In the face of difficulty the affliction purchased by neglect needs formal absence in obtaining a triumphant purification. By God's authority available in condition, this return to vindicate and maintain your true identity is free of charge, just for the asking. Forever in reaching your sanctuary, the incentive from within descends from above applauding your approval. Rejoice in your request granted, for the spiritual refuge you seek will symbolize your gain of control by dedication to preserving your hearts desire. The fulfillment and restoration in positioning your souls residence buries the disturbance once remnant and incomplete.

Remember; lavished rewards await enduring persistence in being spiritually whole.

MY GREATEST longing is to be personal and private with GOD.

I take my mask off and walk with the Lord while living in the confidence and referral of my testimony by Biblical principles. Innermost and intimate cleansing of the mind indicates time to reassemble the care and concern needed from past egotistical and selfish behavior, which then drew attention to detailed failure, and I as clever as I sought to be then, never noticed this menacing and sinister hold of attraction in evil that occupied my every step.

Pledging promise to gain possession of my sanity, I embraced every moment that entered my thought, directing myself to the source and reverence of divinity in placing my cause nearer in appealing for assembly. Resurrecting my spirit to God's authority and raising my level of faith to no retreat, I find here I belong and here I will stay until my dying day.

Prayer gives belief a degree of remarkable ownership to be in the likeness of him.

THE POWER of LIFE

The power of life should be lived in the fear of him to love him.

The evil exchange has made us less of what God has wanted us to become. Taking time for prayer to be within yourself and living in the Gospel will support in faith the truth and meaning of God's word. Holy art thou, precious is thy name, believe in him and you will receive the blessing of eternal fortune.

His powerful and understanding grace permits and interprets the reality in knowing and experiencing, what exactly is offered by his blood. To leave your calling card in true faith and assisting where the wounded have fallen, sets precedence in performing his work for redemption to fulfill the needs of a vacant soul. Providing and nurturing the hunger for souls that have lost their way, will display the power within to reach in and beyond self-help.

Your reason and purpose is to be as one, to become whole in the eyes of God, while placing the word in and around your fellow neighbor.

ASK in Jesus name, and it will be given unto you.

TAKE ALL the fences away, and support a just cause called JOY.

REJOICING in joy leads to divine glory permanently reaching the summit of existence, and is as walking in spirit. Words in deed test trials in faith where joy is reserved by being in Christ and this gives an unlimited well of joy. True joy permeates from the commander of common grace, his matrix of pleasure flows throughout with a listful liberation of joy.

Joy of the flesh is the desire of the weak at heart, causing lust to never cease, and ending so called joy with grief. (Adverse trials of tyranny if exercised will counterfeit joy and only satisfy the despotic ruler Satan.) Rejoice within your joy, even if it seems unjust. I have decided to use the honesty of my soul as I wept sorely in the agony of my fear. When I came to realize I have nothing to loose, life's choices became easier and in knowing that the light does excel while in his presence, so why would I sit in darkness and deny myself this joy. The death of my age is not the death of my morals, for God's answer is to place vertical choices in my sight for a service to Christ, and not in the brink of mystery. As it is said; the Bible will out live its pallbearers, so for my significant passage of faith I say old news is news to new people as reborn. I find my darkest moment is my brightest time at the present. A perfect example is my un-erring wisdom I placed on the verge of darker moments. The grit and courage I deprived my passage of faith, totally depreciated the lessons learned then. Joy now has replaced my sorrow with the agony of a welcoming defeat. AMEN

YOUR TOOL the WORD of GOD

Purchasing your pardon from sin sets seed to the power within.

By self-surrender of thy will your accepted power within is your associate, the Holy Spirit. It took myself forty years to be broken and I am prepared to remold my understanding and bask in my inheritance. I have disavowed, renounced and yielded my will to the power and authority of God's will. The power within must be coherent in mind, orderly and intelligible. (Second Timothy-chapter one, verse seven); For God has not given us the spirit of fear, but of power and love of a sound mind. When there is no particular reason in purpose or plan in one's life, radicalism most likely will encompass its definition without a solid conclusion to reality, building a foundation of regret.

Unveil in mind the authentic authority in God where time itself has infinite meaning now and forevermore. The duration of your stay as a worldly figure reflects on your faith to proceed by determination of your actions toward salvation. We will all perish at one point in time, but to leave a legacy stamped by God's approval is your gift in return to life.

JESUS LOVES YOU and so do I

I ask you, have you taken the time to listen and hear the snowfall?

Have you finally let go of the tug of war between God's needs and the selfish needs

that bind us to plummet and maroon our spiritual nutriment.

SPIRITUALISM is the foundation of our physical world and is the reflection of

our earning's, don't be isolated from God's marketplace. The provision of Jesus becomes

in the fullness of time and by faith our eminent inheritance preserves our infinite value

and sovereign cause. The fact is mistakes will be made and a compass for our guidance is

available through Jesus Christ as our role model in human value. Take the sleigh ride

through the vast and immense mountains of heaven while throwing a cast net onto the

time capsule of regret. Wandering in a baseless idiotic meander through the desert of time

only fortifies the delay in reaching the pure at heart in waiting.

OPEN DOOR

A balcony beyond the stars, a gallery of light fused and merrily mixed in with a galaxy consisting of the finest dust that will bind the mold to authorize the beginning of God's immortal design. Where distance has no say, eternity has no ending, and peace has a place in mind. This is where kindness aired its debut, when joy entered life by marking its territory. Contentment filled every channel that opened its limits, and sunlight embraced the silence that whispered love gently by acceptance.

An awakening pledge promoted promise by commitment, and an appetite for love formed its creation. Sensitivity announced its delicate seed, and desire nourished every moment, while recruiting the excitement of a new beginning. Music then created a window, that dance happened to notice. And while all this presumed its course, God was pleased.

SILENCE found its word, and became our MESSAGE.

UNDERSTAND YOUR ENDING

In learning I have become wiser by assisting in the sound worship of the word. Be the HAMMER in the blacksmiths hand molding rightful purpose, HEAT the flame the soul desires and learn to pray first, not after all flesh results disappoint your expectations. When wrong judgment interferes the work of good intent causing dead results in your expectations, and when exhausted and fruitless, understand why!

Prayer opens doors for God's results to prosper and grow beyond expectations. Your feat of courage in acting upon need is to be private and secret with God, not in the open as displayed by the hypocrites and Pharisees for their own recognition for themselves. When you are secluded in prayer God will be the one to reward you in the open by your deed for need.

Learn to set aside self-motives and be a genuine witness to God's word.

SEPARATED

Fame enduring immortality, everlasting eternal life brings in the darkest night to the brightest day. There are vast swarms of souls aching a dull steady pain yearning for eternal fame seeking placement amongst the most pious and devout, they are the weary that exist in idle torment waiting for their inevitable residence, and there is no substitution in standing that can occupy their position from their choice by their decisions that were made.

While physically alive and by choice, you accepting Christ as your savior surrenders your Will to a balanced sense of meaning salvation, which will sensor the ungodly from the imperial kingdoms wishes. Conquered by confusion, a compulsive and irresistible impulse acts to bring another's keeping into place if willing. Heavens space draws all creation into its final destiny, deemed by decree an unmistakable ending empowered by our maker and the cultural warriors at rest, draws this allegiance hereby inscribed to fulfill the existence of life. Understand, once departed there will be no decisions to be made.

YOUR SOUL is YOUR HIDDEN GEM

Your SOUL is your living presence, your ownership to the gift of life.

Your SPIRIT represents your character, such as your spirit of joy, fear, love, and so on.

Your PERSONALITY is in relationship to who you are and how you perceive your individuality and by how you maintain your true identity. The ingredients needed in preserving who you are has a list of many. Trust, wisdom, belief by faith, hope, prayer and choice, just to name a few that safeguard your existence. By faith the strongest of them all, and by accordance to God's wishes, these ingredients are your guidelines to an obedient heart. To understand your physical departure and the message within these ingredients is to invite wisdom by nourishing the knowledge given in your thought. Take an inventory of your souls condition, and understand the accuracy and accountability that fully permits standards to be set in human order. This function is as fidelity and loyalty is to confidence, which in return leads to a strong and upright belief. Get closer to the heart of God, for he will meet you no matter where you are, and remember everything that happens, happens first in mind if the will to want receives the blessings given by an obedient heart. The wealth in understanding our souls restoration I believe can only be obtained by the spirits willingness to surrender, and by having in account a truly broken spirit.

Carl Eric Wahlstedt

MY PRAYER TO YOU

THANKS and BLESSINGS

FATHER thank-you for the food and drink that strengthen our bodies and enables us to carry out the work you give us to do. Thank-you also for those whose work makes food available to us, we are truly grateful. For all worldwide, may their hunger for food and your gracious word, fill their needs. For all the sick and crippled may they find strength to overcome all ailments through your power and glory, and for all the obstacles that they may encounter. Lord we ask you to protect and guide our families and loved one's who are so dear to our heart, and also the one's who protect us in difficult times.

We thank-you God for your highest and most precious sacrifice, to save what was left of mankind through the blood of your only begotten Son, which in return gives us another chance to redeem ourselves as we choose so. On the last days of the last hour we pray that you look upon us with mercy.

For all of us that believe in your precious name, we wait humbly for your return.

AMEN

CEW

Summary

In this inhabited world sabotaged by Satan, we the children of wrath that are captive to an alien prince, seek resolve from fraught and failure. This evil incarnate by means of its perverse power has influenced the latitudes and platitudes by its execution.

This cultural slavery of sin presents its darkness that shadows our rightful inheritance to our attributed worth. Christ was revealed through his fathers word by which a testimony through his sacrifice enables us to be firm in our faith as by witness. Jesus walks in our shadows so that we can become heirs of our inherited right, (life ever-lasting). Remember upon the turrets of time our reflection becomes the decision and direction we have agreed upon. If we honor his benevolent gift then surely a prophetic voice will whisper in high-spirited joy as to the decision entrusted beyond our control. You are not to be refused if your element of digestion satisfies the confession of your humility. There is the treachery that lurks in arms reach that disables the spiritual relationship and spawns its ill-mannered reliance. Penetrable as blame shows the way, voluntary suffering or penance then chases the cure. Savor the promise given on the provision deserved, and deny the insignificant soul you have become. There is no other name given among men by which you can be saved, few will find the way of the cross, but all who labor in JUST, he will give rest be assured.

The earth will someday dissolve my heart, but my soul it cannot receive. Secure your place within your heart and be the fabric of your faith. Don't be held idle by a cold stone heart that falters by the direction of neglect. This is important; either by triumph or tragedy your internal encouragement invites you as a new member to the archway in answer if willing. Be sure of your redemption, be strengthened by it, and be saved by salvation. For God is the potter, while Christ is the potter's-wheel that puts your burden at the foot of his altar. (Revelation 22-verse 14) Blessed are those who do His commandments, that they may have the right to the tree of life, and enter through the gates into the city, which mean's, blessed are those who are not forgotten, but who daily confess their sin that they might be cleaned.

The son's of disobedience that execute darkness while believing in their success neglect their obligation by shying away without Christ as savior and become encircled by doom. Holy fear then by displeasure ignites the internal flame, unveiling the announcement of judgment. Only peace within heralds the entrance privately sharing time alone spent with Jesus. Your life forevermore begins with Christ when your faith resides in Christ.

This I want you to know; that in the beginning the word became flesh and dwelt among us and shined its face in its awakening. How splendid the window of reality would be to the unknown believer, if only a step toward understanding God's word would prioritize his or her meaning to life. Without true spiritual value the principles to life in which we observe and should live by would only wither and disappear in thought. If anyone acknowledges that Jesus is the Son of God, then God lives in him and he in God.

Are you filled with un-forgiveness? When reading scripture don't design its message, as you want it to be understood, but read it for the understanding that the meaning behind the message is God's word. When guilt nourishes suffering by being filled with un-forgiveness, remember guilt is of your own doing and the wrongdoing will eat at the inner core of misplacement, placing misery as its host. But also in respect by suffering, God allows those to suffer that he cares about most so that they may understand the true meaning of his forgiveness.

The personal relationship that formulates just cause and affect can only be found through the artery of righteous intent by commitment to change and by a privatized relationship with the founder and father of life God the Almighty, and the savior to everlasting life his son, Jesus Christ. Rightful cause and affect can then produce confidence in belief and rid the un-rightful suggestion that misguides trust by refusing forgiveness or sought thereof.

God be with you.